Series Editor: Alan Ware
University of Oxford

# gender and the vote in britain
## in britain

### beyond the gender gap?

Rosie Campbell

D0556817

© Rosie Campbell

First published by the ECPR Press in 2006

The ECPR Press is the publishing imprint of the European Consortium for
Political Research (ECPR), an independent, scholarly association, which supports
and encourages the training, research and cross-national cooperation of political
scientists in institutions throughout Europe and beyond. The ECPR's Central
Services are located at the University of Essex, Wivenhoe Park,
Colchester, CO4 3SQ, UK

Typeset in Times 10pt by the ECPR Press
Printed and bound in the UK by the University of Essex Print Centre

British Library Cataloguing in Publication Data
A catalogue record for this book is available from the British Library

ISBN: 0-9547966-9-1
ISBN 13: 978-0-9547966-9-3

monographs

The ECPR Monographs series is published by the ECPR Press, the publishing imprint of the European Consortium for Political Research (ECPR).

As an independent, scholarly, institution, one of the ECPR's objectives is to facilitate research in political science among European universities. To that end, the ECPR has developed a strong publishing portfolio since the 1970s.

The policy to extend that portfolio by launching its own publishing imprint was discussed by the Executive Committee of the ECPR in 2002, and the decision to proceed was taken in early 2003.

It was decided that the first two series to be published under the imprint should be complementary. The ECPR Classics series facilitates scholarly access to significant works from earlier eras of political science by re-publishing books that have been out of print. The ECPR believes this will enable contemporary students and researchers to develop their own work more effectively.

The ECPR Monographs series publishes major new research in all sub-disciplines of political science including revised versions of manuscripts that were originally submitted as PhD theses, as well as manuscripts from established members of the profession.

Alan Ware
Editor, ECPR Classics and ECPR Monographs
Worcester College, Oxford University, UK

For Ian Campbell
(Something to argue about)

# contributors

Rosie Campbell
Lecturer in Research Methods, School of Politics and Sociology
Birkbeck College, University of London

Kristi Winters
Senior Researcher for the British Election Study 2005
Department of Government, University of Essex

# acknowledgements

The completion of this book depended upon the help of a great bunch of friends and colleagues. I am very grateful for all of their support. None of them is responsible for any errors or clumsy prose. I would particularly like to thank Joni Lovenduski and Peter John for their words of wisdom and patience. Eric Tanenbaum kindly read an early version of chapter three. To Chris Wlezien, Geoff Evans and those who attended the Nuffield research seminar: thank you for your suggestions. David Sanders and Anne Phillips were PhD examiners from heaven. The British Academy funded the qualitative research presented in Chapter four. Thanks also to Alan Ware for all of his advice, to Sarah Childs, Kristi Winters and Rainbow Murray for discussing these things with me and to Isla Campbell for reading the first draft. Finally, I'm very grateful to Bernie Aryeetey for keeping me smiling.

# contents

# introduction

Speculation about the way men and women are going to vote is a recurrent feature of media coverage at election time (Stephenson 1997; Norris 1999; Hayes 1997). However, there is no longer a significant gender gap and any reference to a 'women's vote' would be spurious. At an aggregate level the picture of sex and voting in Britain is one of more similarity than difference. In contrast to the United States, where women are significantly more likely to vote for Democratic candidates than men, women and men in Britain vote for the major parties in roughly equal numbers. However, behind the aggregate similarity lies a complex pattern of gender differences that combine to contribute to election outcomes. Different sub-groups of men and women vote for different parties. For example, there is literature which indicates that younger women are now more likely to vote for the Labour Party than younger men (Norris 1999).

A gender gap in vote choice could manifest itself in two ways. There may be a gender gap in party of vote or there may be a *motivational* gender gap in vote choice, where men and women vote for the same party for different reasons. Research has shown that there are gender differences in political attitudes (Jelen, Thomas and Wilcox 1994). However, there has been little systematic analysis of how gender differences in attitudes impact upon voting behaviour. Analysis of the 2001 and 1997 British Election Studies (BES) suggests that men and women, and different groups of men and women, do weigh issues differently when deciding how to vote. In addition to sub-group gender gaps, this book finds evidence of motivational sex and gender gaps.

This book attempts to answer the question 'in what way and to what extent are women's political preferences, as expressed in voting behaviour, different to men's?'. To answer it, the extensive United States gender gap literature is used for hypothesis generation. The gender gap in the United States, where more women than men vote for Democratic presidential candidates, has been evident since 1980. Until 2005 there has been no evidence of an equivalent gender gap at an aggregate level in Britain. MORI opinion poll data from the 2005 British general election suggests that such a gap may have emerged in Britain at this point.[1] Therefore it is timely to consider whether the underlying causes of the US gender gap also contribute to gender differences in voting behaviour in Britain.

## METHODS

The chapters of this book are designed to work in sequence from indirect to direct effects on party of vote. Models of voting behaviour often obscure gender differences, which usually involve complex indirect effects. For example, sex may interact with parenthood to influence attitudes and then vote. This is because, in British society, women undertake a larger proportion of parenting than men and may, therefore, have a particular interest in childcare policies. Women who are mothers might be more likely to vote for parties who pledge to increase the provision of childcare. Simply including the sex variable into an otherwise complete model of voting behaviour would not uncover this relationship, because the difference would not be between all women and all men but instead between mothers (and those anticipating motherhood) and the rest of the electorate.

Estimating the impact of background characteristics on vote choice is problematic. If the sex variable is simply plugged into an already complete model of vote it has little theoretic power. Achen provides one possible solution to this problem,

> when researchers are being theoretically serious, demographics should be discarded...Age, social class, and other background factors...may provide a serviceable summary for purely descriptive purposes. But they may not belong to explanatory equations (Achen 1992: 198–209).

An alternative approach would be to suggest a structural relationship between the variables. For example, social characteristics can have an impact on voters' experiences and beliefs, which may, in turn, impact upon vote. Theoretically, therefore, the fact that an individual voter is a mother who works full-time might shape her experiences and lead her to prioritise child care; her role as a carer may influence the issues which are most salient to her, perhaps education or healthcare. In this formula, the demographics that designate life experiences to members of particular groups, or holders of certain attributes, are theorised to have an indirect effect on vote.

There have been a number of influential critiques of the research methods commonly employed in studies of voting behaviour in Britain (Catt 1996; Dunleavy 1990; Evans, Heath, and Lalljee 1996; Scarbrough 2000). Dunleavy summarises one of the weaknesses common within many voting studies.

> Frequently it has been thought legitimate to simply put a large number of supposedly equivalent and independent 'variables' into a large pot and then let the computer select those which correlate most closely with alignments – a method which underpins the frequently rediscovered claim that issue attitudes 'explain' far more of the variance in voting than social background variables. The fact that most social background variables are demonstrably prior to vote, both logically and empirically, while most attitudinal indicators are not, apparently carries no weight (Dunleavy 1990: 456).

Current research is not as inductively driven as the approach described above. It is now usual for researchers to test theoretically driven models, and procedures such as stepwise regression, are widely discredited. However, Dunleavy's description does highlight how difficult it is to specify relationships between independent variables using regression analysis.

There are a number of mechanisms for assessing the strength of indirect effects; their potential for specifying indirect relationships between sex, attitude and vote are considered here. One such mechanism is to introduce batteries of interaction terms.[2] Thus, we might include terms for sex and age, sex and class, sex and income, sex, age and attitude, and so on. However, modelling the relationship between vote and background characteristics, such as sex, requires an enormous array of interactions, which tend to produce problems of multicollinearity.

An alternative method for introducing causal order that is sometimes employed in the study of voting behaviour is the 'funnel of causality'. The 'funnel of causality' was first conceived by Campbell *et al.* in *The American Voter* (Campbell *et al.* 1960). It was a heuristic designed to separate long- and short-term influences on vote choice.[3] In Miller and Shanks's research the term 'funnel of causality' is used to describe the process whereby variables are sifted into blocks, according to their distance from vote choice. Direct and indirect effects are calculated by producing a series of regression coefficients with an increasing number of control variables. Campbell *et al.* point out that the funnel of causality has a 'strong deterministic flavour', (xii). The funnel of causality is more sophisticated than throwing all of the variables into a single regression equation because, in multiple regression, the independent variables compete on equal terms for significance, regardless of their internal relationships. However, the funnel of causality heuristic is deterministic and descriptive rather than analytic, because its employment forces the researcher to make fundamental assumptions about the relationships between the variables, the accuracy of which cannot be tested.

The limitations of the methods outlined above suggest that the best approach to modelling indirect effects or background characteristics might be to conduct analysis on separate groups. A strong case for employing models for men and women separately has been made by Clarke *et al.* (Clarke *et al.* 2004). In their analysis of the gender gap in presidential approval ratings they state:

> The hypotheses that gender differences in presidential approval reflect process heterogeneity rather than simple level heterogeneity in the effects of economic evaluations require that we employ a general strategy of testing rival models of the dynamics of presidential approval for men and women separately (40).

The potential differences between the sexes described by Clarke *et al.* as either 'process' or 'level' heterogeneity have been described elsewhere as 'attitudinal' or 'motivational' gender gaps (Steel 2003) or as 'positional' or 'structural' approaches (Sapiro and Conover 1997). The analysis in this research will proceed by applying models to sub-samples of men and women.

The chapters are designed to work together, in sequence, following the principal steps of the funnel of causality, to provide a comprehensive model of gender and vote in Britain. Chapter three models the relationship between gender and political attitudes. Chapter four is an analysis of gender and turnout and is a logical precursor to considering party of vote. Chapter five reflects upon the relationship between electoral context, gender and vote choice. Chapter six looks at the electoral context, with an analysis of gender and economic attitudes and gender and evaluations of parties and leaders. Finally, Chapter seven is a case study of the 2005 British general election using focus group data and quantitative analysis. The final chapter draws some conclusions from the previous analysis.

## NOTES

1  MORI Final aggregate analysis from the pooled campaign surveys, 16 May 2005, Total N. 17,595 (www.mori.com).

2  Interaction terms allow the researcher to specify a relationship between independent variables. Jaccard, James, Robert Turrisi, and Choi Kwan, 1996, *Interaction Effects in Multiple Regression*, London: Sage.

3  The concept was further refined by Shanks and Miller in 'The New American Voter.' Miller, Warren, and Merrill J. Shanks, 1996, *The New American Voter*, Cambridge: Harvard University Press.

# chapter one | why gender and voting behaviour? feminist theory and other accounts

This chapter outlines why the study of gender and voting behaviour is important from a feminist perspective. It locates the research within a body of feminist empirical and theoretical literature and introduces the key concepts used in this book. The chapter also develops an approach that looks beyond the 'gender gap' and considers sub-group differences between the sexes as well as motivational gender gaps in political behaviour.

The chapter begins with a brief introduction to feminist theory and method and then goes on to consider the research question and its relation to feminist research. Theoretical models of gender difference are then utilised to develop testable hypotheses. I then review United States gender gap research. In the process of collating the literature it became apparent that the explanatory power of the analysis of the gender gap in the United States was dependent upon the operationalisation of a concept of gender. The distinction between sex and gender is discussed and then applied to a review of the gender-gap literature.

## FEMINIST THEORY AND METHOD

Feminist theories of gender difference can help us to develop models of gender and voting behaviour. The application of feminist theory has radical implications for empirical research. Firstly, feminists challenge the content of existing research paradigms by asking 'where are the women?' and apply a gendered focus to historically androcentric disciplines. Secondly, and more radically, some feminist perspectives challenge the use of scientific methods altogether. The following section locates this research within feminist empirical literature, using feminist theory for hypothesis generation, but rejects some of the more radical claims about what constitutes a feminist research programme.

### Feminism and the scientific method

Historical and theoretical reflection has given feminist theorists insights into the structures of patriarchy and the consequent nature of women's subordination. These insights have been applied to both the content and application of scientific research, highlighting the androcentrism of both what is researched and how it is researched. The second wave of feminism encouraged a critical review of hierarchical and formal scientific research procedures (Harding 1986; Harding 1991). The consciousness-raising groups of the seventies provided a new forum for political discussion between women, challenging the public/private split that had previously governed research practice. The liberal assertion of a clear divide between public and private life disadvantaged women. Women's concerns were often defined as private; therefore, they could not demand political or public solutions to their concerns, and were not deemed appropriate for social science research. In this way issues such as domestic violence were obscured from the research agenda.

Second-wave feminists declared that 'the personal is political' and sought to bring previously 'private' matters on to the political agenda. Following this second wave, some of the demands of feminist research methods appeared to conflict with those of scientific research. Ann Oakely asserted that for a feminist to interview a woman using a pre-determined interview schedule was morally indefensible (Oakely 1972). In response, Randall suggested that the implication of Oakely's standpoint was that feminists should only undertake certain kinds of social research (Randall 1991). To accept Oakely's constraint limits the scope of feminist research too much, by ignoring many arenas where women are found but do not, in general, receive equal treatment to men. Such limitation occurs because the kind of research recommended by Oakely requires a sympathetic and responsive researcher. Oakely's demands require feminist researchers to refrain from studying research questions where a rigorous application of the scientific practice of comparison is essential. For example, in order to understand whether men and women think about political issues in the same way we must ask the same questions and see if we elicit the same answers. Oakely's prescription might be well suited to research into rape and violent crime but has a limited application. There should be some provision, therefore, for a feminist research agenda that recognises the male bias present in many research techniques without simultaneously negating the principles of good research design.

The approach undertaken in this book is to use the feminist research technique of asking 'where are the women?' without rejecting scientific methods, to review a range of voting behaviour studies and then to apply quantitative and qualitative data analysis techniques to answer feminist research questions.

## Sex and gender
Feminist theory helps us to make a distinction between sex and gender. Contemporary feminist research is concerned with gender and not sex differences. Many feminist theorists base their claims on a notion of a women's interest or experience. However, few contemporary theorists try to provide a universal description of women's experiences; instead they outline the institutions and practices that impact on women's lives, with consequences that differ, depending on their interaction with other factors such as race or class (Fenstermaker and West 2002).

When thinking about men and women and electoral behaviour it is important to use the concept of gender (Lovenduski 1998). The sex variable cross-cuts almost all other demographic variables and interacts with them to create gendered patterns of political behaviour. Examining the sex variable in isolation from other factors can lead the researcher to make essentialising claims about the nature of women and men. Joni Lovenduski describes how to undertake research into gender in political science (Lovenduski 2001).

> 'Gender' is defined as characteristic of both women and men and is expressed in the differences between the sexes that result from the division of labour between women and men…gender is not a synonym for 'sex' and any examination of gender politics needs to consider both femininity and masculinity (Lovenduski 2001: 180).

The division of labour described by Lovenduski refers mainly to the distribution of caring work and women's role as mothers. The sexual division of non-paid caring work impacts upon the distribution of other paid employment. The relationship between care and employment is explored in more detail in Chapter five.

The nature of the distinction between sex and gender has been the focus of a fraught debate within feminism. Any researcher wading through the literature attempting to operationalise the two terms will find that there is no immediate solution. For the purposes of this research sex is defined as biological sex. Sex is operationalised in the surveys used here by asking respondents whether they are a man or a woman. For our purposes gender is operationalised as the interaction between biological sex and other locations of identity. Gender is not conceived as dichotomous but as a scale of attributes from masculine to feminine. Women are more likely to possess feminine attributes but these do not belong to them exclusively. Gender is operationalised here by analysing differences between the sexes within sub-groups. Sub-group analysis allows us to avoid making essentialising claims about 'all women' or 'all men'. Thus we might test for gender differences amongst professional men and women in isolation from other occupational sectors. It would be preferable to use a gender scale, rather than the binary distinction of sex and then subdividing it into sub-groups. However, such a scale is not available within the British Election Studies (BES) series. Gender scales have been used elsewhere in political and social science research (Withey 2003). Julie Withey has operationalised a two-dimensional concept of gender to assess whether 'masculinity and femininity are coherent explanatory variables which together will provide a link to defining and explaining sex differences' in political behaviour (Withey 2003: 11).

## WHY IS THE RESEARCH IMPORTANT?

Addressing the overarching research question, 'in what way and to what extent are women's political preferences, as expressed in voting behaviour, different to men's?' will add to the body of feminist social science research, as well as contributing to electoral research. The findings of this research should contribute to the debate about whether women have specific perspectives or interests that remain unarticulated in the political system. Evidence that men and women have different interests would be pertinent to the debate about the under-representation of women in British politics. Feminist scholarship in political theory and political science has demonstrated that women are under-represented in public life. The under-representation of women in parliament has been criticised as unjust but it is also sometimes argued that only women legislators can provide substantive representation of women. In an attempt to establish whether women have interests that are generally unarticulated in the political system, feminist researchers have investigated the behaviour of representatives and identified the way women representatives behave once they are in office (Childs 2002; Dahlerup 1988; Karvonen and Selle 1995). If women representatives deliver a women's perspective or represent women's interests, then the substantive under-representation of women is important.

An alternative to the study of political elites, described above, is to study the attitudes and behaviours of mass publics, e.g. the electorate. Studies of mass publics are bottom-up and allow us to test theories at the citizen level. Electoral research provides an opportunity for collecting data on the attitudes and behaviours of mass publics with a large sample size. Large sample sizes permit rigorous quantitative analysis and allow us to test hypotheses generated from feminist theories within sub-groups. This study of voting behaviour can complement elite studies by assessing the gender dimensions of political attitudes and behaviour within the electorate. If electoral behaviour and elite behaviour have gender dimensions then there might be evidence to support claims for equal political representation of the sexes. Evidence of gendered political attitudes within the electorate would have implications for questions of accountability. Such evidence would suggest that the political demands of men and women might differ and could provide support for an element of Anne Phillips's argument for a 'politics of presence' (Phillips 1995).

In *The Politics of Presence* Anne Phillips develops an argument in support of quota systems, which ensure that political parties choose women candidates. It is her contention that women's interests cannot be sufficiently articulated through patriarchal political systems. She states that there are 'women's issues', or experiences particular to women that can only be addressed by women themselves. Phillips suggests that the precise nature of women's interests will not be known until a debate, between women, takes place within the public arena. Policies must be initiated by female politicians and, until they are, the issues themselves will not be clearly defined. A significant number of women politicians are needed if these issues are to be raised and defined because, until a threshold number of women hold positions of power, women will form a *skewed group* (Dahlerup 1988). Drude Dahlerup defines a skewed group as one where the minority is represented in the chamber by less than 15 per cent. When women representatives form a skewed group they will be treated as tokens and discouraged from expressing the needs of the minority. Women will be unable to form alliances with other women representatives. When women form a skewed group, in order to further their careers and to perceive themselves as successful, they may tend to adopt priorities predetermined by the patriarchal nature of institutions. Phillips highlights the biased nature of the selection procedures operated by political parties in many Western European nations to explain why affirmative action is required in order for the threshold number of female candidates to be met. The research in this book will contribute to the debate about the political representation of women. If political preferences are found to be gendered, then effective political representation ought to reflect these different perspectives in order to provide substantive representation of women.

Quota systems are not without their opponents. Hannah Pitkin used the image of the 'slippery slope' to defend traditional representative democracy from a decline into mirror representation (Pitkin 1967). She insisted that the purpose of representative democracy, as opposed to direct democracy, is to delegate representative functions to others. Representatives are obliged to protect the interests of all of their constituents, regardless of their physical qualities. Through the representative function legislators are directly accountable to their constituents. Pitkin argues that, in the case of 'mirror' representation, accountability would be lost in confusion. She suggests that representatives could claim to know their constituents' interests without communication because of an essentialised understanding of what it is to be human. Phillips finds this argument unconvincing because women have a distinct position within society. For example, women tend to be employed in low-paid jobs and hold the primary responsibility for unpaid and caring work. These experiences lead to specific interests or perspectives that will not be adequately addressed by a political system that is characterised by the dramatic under-representation of women in numerical or proportional terms. In a just society, one would expect the personal qualities of representatives to be randomly distributed; where this distribution is significantly skewed in favour of one group the distribution cannot be described as benign (Phillips 1994). It is argued, therefore, that it does matter who our representatives are. Let us move on to consider the representation of women in Britain.

In Britain, women are under-represented in parliament. Since 1997 there has been a dramatic increase in the number of women Members of Parliament (MPs). However, after the 2005 general election women still constituted only 19.8 per cent of MPs (Campbell and Lovenduski 2005). If political attitudes or preferences are delineated by sex or gender in the electorate then the under-representation of women and over-representation of men in parliament will bias the political system in favour of male attitudes or preferences and this, from a feminist research perspective, is one reason why the research undertaken in this book is important.[1]

## THEORETICAL PERSPECTIVES AND HYPOTHESIS GENERATION

To provide a sound research design, hypotheses must be developed from theoretical models prior to data analysis. As is usual with quantitative secondary data analysis, it is important to avoid data dredging because it may lead to the discovery of spurious sex or gender effects without any basis from which to infer their significance. The specific difficulty to be addressed is the subtle nature of gender effects and the fine balance needed to avoid essentialising claims without 'washing out' gender differences altogether. The review of gender and voting behaviour research in this chapter and the review of mainstream British voting behaviour research in Chapter two, will explore the way that gender is operationalised. An aim of the two chapters is to establish how to undertake gendered analysis without making essentialist claims about all men and all women. Theories of gender difference are taken from feminist empirical research and feminist political theory. A review of the models produced by the two sources will be conducted and used to create testable hypotheses.

Feminist theorists provide models that illustrate the different experiences of women and men. Some theorists have emphasised the impact of mothering on the psyches of the sexes, causing women to stress caring for others as opposed to developing an isolated sense of the self (Chodorow 1978; Diamond and Hartsock 1981; Ruddick 1989).

Chodorow claims that the psyches of the sexes are determined by the traditional division of labour. The socialisation process, where women are present in the home caring for children and men are absent and active in the public sphere, leads women to prioritise relationships and to conceive of themselves as connected to others, whereas men are more likely to think of themselves as discrete individuals because in order to achieve manhood, men learn that they must separate from their mother.

> A female cannot maintain in any simple way the distinction Freud saw as central to human existence – the clear disjunction between me and not me... Psychoanalytic evidence suggests that as a result of these early experiences, women tend to define themselves relationally while men are more likely to form a sense of self as separate and disconnected from the world (Diamond and Hartsock 1981: 718).

Chodorow argues that these differences are likely to persist until men and women undertake dual parenting. There are implications of Chodorow's analysis for the study of gender and voting behaviour. If mothering does have a significant impact upon the formation of the psyches of the sexes, leading women to think relationally and men to think abstractly, then we would expect the way men and women think and talk about politics to be similarly differentiated.

Another feminist theorist who focuses upon the impact of mothering is Sara Ruddick (Ruddick 1989). Ruddick claims that the daily work of mothering encourages women to think about society and politics from a caring and altruistic perspective; men do not develop the same compassionate nature because their daily life is less concerned with the care of others.

Carol Gilligan's 'ethics of care' also suggests gendered attitudes to politics. Gilligan claimed that women's moral development may not involve the same processes as men's (Gilligan 1982). Gilligan's *In a Different Voice* is a critique of traditional theories of moral development, especially the work of Lawrence Kohlberg. Kohlberg used the behavioural patterns of boys to develop a scale of moral development. Kohlberg then used the boys' scale to assess the development of girls, finding them lacking. Gilligan suggests that there might be a corollary to the ethics of justice (the male ethics), which is the 'ethics of care' and is more commonly found in the morality of girls and women than men, although not exclusively so. Although Gilligan describes different processes evident in the moral development of men and women, she indicates towards the end of *In a Different Voice*, that eventually men and women achieve a similar understanding of morality, based upon both an 'ethics of care' and justice. However, in the United States gender-gap literature, the Gilligan model is usually reduced to a dichotomy between the psyches of men and women. Such a reduction aids operationalisation of the theory into measurement terms and has been utilised to produce some insightful research in the United States.

The theories, outlined above, have been used by researchers to develop hypotheses about the potential differences between men and women's political attitudes and behaviour. The theories of Chodorow, Ruddick and Gilligan all have different bases and implications but they can all be operationalised to suggest that women will be more likely than men to think about politics in a connected, relational manner that will lead them to prioritise social welfare provision rather than individualistic market solutions. Such hypotheses might be:

- Women's political preferences are more likely to be based on an interest in social issues, whereas men are more likely to be chiefly concerned with pocket-book politics.
- Women prefer spending on education and health services to tax reduction.

These hypothesises have been used, both explicitly and implicitly, by researchers in the United States to compare the 'ethics of care' model to rational choice explanations for the gender gap (Box-Steffensmeir, DeBoef and Lin 1997; Chaney, Alvarez and Nagler 1998; Kornhauser 1987; Kornhauser 1997; Welch and Hibbing 1992). These particular articles are discussed in detail later in this chapter. However, it is worth taking a moment here to consider whether feminist theories and rational choice theories are in fact mutually exclusive.

## FEMINISM AND RATIONAL CHOICE THEORY

A number of articles on the gender gap in the United States compare 'ethics of care' to rational choice explanations. The 'ethics of care' argument is usually simplified to argue that women are more likely to vote for Democratic candidates because of an altruistic concern for other members of society. Rational choice explanations suggest that women vote for Democratic candidates because they are more likely than men to be the beneficiaries of public spending. There are two problems with comparing rational choice to 'ethics of care' explanations. First the two are not mutually exclusive and second they tend to produce similar hypotheses.

There are a number of feminist critiques of rational choice theories (Andersen 2002; Cudd 2002; England and Kilbourne 1990a; England and Kilbourne 1990b). Before proceeding to the feminist critiques it is useful to attempt to briefly define rational choice theory (RCT). Rational choice theory is an umbrella term for a group of theoretical models that attempt to explain how people choose, including public choice theory, social choice theory, game theory and rational actor models (Green and Shapiro 1994). In RCT the individual is a rational actor, who expects consequences from his/her actions, and will choose to act in a way that will maximise his/her expected benefit or utility from the outcome (Anzer 2004). It is an assumption of RCT that individuals will act on the basis of their self-interest. However, self-interest in RCT can be described as non-tuism, that is simply that an individual's motivations cannot be accounted for by the preferences of others (Cudd 2002: 399). However, when rational choice explanations are employed in studies of the gender gap in the United States self-interest is usually narrowly defined as personal material benefits; this operationalisation is also sometimes called 'thick' rationality.

Elizabeth Andersen asks whether feminists should reject RCT (Andersen 2002). Her conclusion is that RCTs that utilise 'thick' descriptions of rationality are irreconcilable with feminist concerns because of their failure to recognise the fundamentally connected nature of humanity. She states that 'the theory in conceiving of rationality in terms of cold, instrumental, selfish, quantitative calculation, relies on a gender polarized conceptual scheme' (Andersen 2002: 369). However, Andersen's critique is levelled at RCT as if it is intended to be an explanation of all human behaviour. When RCT is employed, particularly in empirical research, it is generally not used to attempt to explain all human behaviour but is used as a model of a particular aspect of a specific context. Thus, it might be employed to generate testable hypotheses that lead to explicit predictions that are forced to compete with other models in quantitative analysis.

Paula England and Barbara Kilbourne base their criticism of RCT on its conception of a separate-self (England and Kilbourne 1990a). They define RCT as a sub-field of neoclassical economics and therefore engage in a broad discussion of its general characteristics. England and Kilbourne list feminisms' multiple attacks upon the separate-self, including Carol Gilligan's 'ethics of care' and Nancy Chodorow's psychoanalytic feminist theory. England and Kilbourne then analyse the assumptions of RCT, starting with selfishness. They acknowledge that selfishness is not necessarily an essential assumption of RCT but, nevertheless, it is usually employed because without it 'determinant predictions of the type which economists derive mathematically are often impossible' (England and Kilbourne 1990a: 162). Thus, they embark upon a critique of thick rationality. They demonstrate the masculinity of the selfishness assumption because it is likely to motivate separate rather than connected selves.

This critique of thick rationality is sound if one attempts to use RCT as a general theory of human behaviour. However England and Kilbourne fail to recognise that the predictive forms of RCT they criticise are model generating rather than general theories. Thus, they might be used to explain an individual decision to vote, or not vote, or to cooperate with another politician, or not. Such predictive models do not generally attempt to explain the structure of the institutional context and they are intended to help answer only small empirical questions. The goal of such research is to build up knowledge of specific contexts that can contribute to an accumulating understanding of human behaviour. Thus, rational choice explanations can reasonably be used as competing alternatives to 'ethics of care' explanations. However, the division of labour between the two explanations is further problematised by the fact that they are in fact not mutually exclusive. An 'ethics of care' could be incorporated into rational choice explanations as long as mothers are not considered to be indiscriminate altruists.

Rational choice and 'ethics of care' explanations are not mutually exclusive because their separation depends upon the assumption that rational choice explanations exclude altruism. Altruistic acts, whereby individuals do not expect the beneficiaries of their actions to reciprocate directly but instead consider themselves members of a society where others will behave altruistically, are perfectly compatible with rational choice explanations (Ware 1990). An individual may help their neighbour in the belief that at some future point they may need help from a different member of the local community. Thus, selfless acts are undertaken in a context where they combine to create trust and reciprocity. An 'ethics of care' explanation is only incompatible with rational choice if it believed that women will be indiscriminate altruists, that is that they will continue to undertake selfless acts indefinitely even when others behave selfishly towards them. Thus, they should be willing to continue to pay higher taxes for welfare benefits even if other members of society free ride on their generosity and pay no taxes. It seems unlikely that the 'ethics of care' explanation would require such a strong conception of altruism. Instead the 'ethics of care' thesis simply requires that women are more likely to think about others when making political choices than men. Thus, it is difficult to maintain a separation between the two approaches. In fact, Cudd claims 'nothing in the theory suggests that one cannot, would not, or ought not spend one's resources on whatever one likes, including children and significant others in need' (Cudd 2002: 406).

In addition to the fact that rational choice and 'ethics of care' explanations may not be mutually exclusive the two theories also tend to produce similar hypotheses about men and women's behaviour. An 'ethics of care' account would suggest that women would prefer to payer higher taxes if the proceeds were to be spent on health and education. A rational choice account might suggest instead that women who are, or expect to be, mothers would prefer higher taxation if it were linked to increased spending on education. The difference between the accounts is that from an 'ethics of care' perspective most women should prefer higher taxes and higher public spending, whereas from the rational choice perspective only women with a material interest would prefer higher taxes and higher public spending. Thus, the most plausible way to test the two approaches is to compare the political attitudes and behaviours of mothers and other women, or other members of the electorate. In practice the two approaches are extremely difficult to untangle because a large number of women are either mothers or might expect to be mothers, thus leaving little variation in the independent variable.

The previous discussion has highlighted the potential problems encountered when employing competing explanations for gender difference. The general approach of this book will be to test the hypotheses outlined without determining whether the 'ethics of care' or rational choice account is the best explanation. Chapter five will consider the impact of background characteristics, including parenthood, and will attempt to establish whether mothers have different political preferences from other members of the electorate, thus providing a weak test of the two theories. Chapter seven includes focus-group data which will enable an analysis of whether men and women talk about politics using a self-interest based individualistic language or whether they tend to talk about others they know and society in general.

**The gender gap in the United States**
In the United States there is a clear aggregate gender gap, which researchers are seeking to explain. The modern gender gap in the United States, whereby women vote for the Democrats in greater numbers than men, has been evident since 1980. In Britain the question is not 'why does the gap exist?' but 'does the gap exist and, if so, is it likely to expand?'. Gender and voting behaviour has been extensively analysed in the United States; much of this research has attempted to test theoretical explanations for gender difference and has developed sophisticated methods for analysing data from a feminist perspective. Thus, research from the United States is an abundant source of hypotheses and potential research designs for studies of gender and voting in other countries. The review of the gender-gap literature, alongside the review of the mainstream voting behaviour literature in Chapter two, helps us to think about how to avoid washing out gender differences without making essentialist claims about all men and all women. The discussion will demonstrate the need to combine examination of aggregate-level sex differences with the analysis of sex differences within sub-groups.

Sub-group analysis helps us to avoid making essentialist claims about all men and all women and to employ a concept of gender rather than sex. One of the most powerful critiques of early second-wave feminism was the way the interests of white middle-class women masqueraded as the interests of all women (Hooks 1982; Hooks 1989). Although women are responsible for caring work within most groups in society, how this translates into attitudes, behaviour and experience will differ. The collective voice of women raised in the second wave of feminism did not address the fact that white middle-class women often collude with patriarchy by employing working-class and/or black women to undertake domestic labour at low rates of pay and with poor job security. The demands of white middle-class women for access to employment, education and childcare did not necessarily consider that working-class women had always participated in paid employment and might like the opportunity to care for their own children. Furthermore the double burden of prejudice faced by black women was not taken into account. Early second-wave feminists were therefore accused of essentialism by ignoring diversity amongst women. Contemporary feminists attempt to overcome this weakness by considering how gender produces multiple and different inequalities within society. Thus, older women might have different interests, needs and experiences of inequality than younger women, as might working-class versus middle-class women or white versus black women. In order to avoid essentialism we can consider sex differences within sub-groups of the population. The following literature review will demonstrate how the failure to consider sub-group differences can undermine gendered analysis.

### Review of studies of the gender gap
In the following section, studies of the gender gap are reviewed and used to generate hypotheses and a model of how to test for gender differences.

Carole Chaney, Michael Alvarez and Jonathan Nagler have produced detailed and insightful research into the gender gap in the United States. They claim that their study of the gender gap adds significantly to the literature because, unlike many other studies, it concerns more than one presidential race (Chaney, Alvarez, and Nagler 1998). Secondly, they contend that previous studies have overemphasised the role of partisanship. Thirdly, they claim to be able to offer a more insightful analysis because they do not attempt to rely on single-issue explanations (Chaney, Alvarez and Nagler 1998: 313). Several competing explanations for the gender gap are tested and regression analysis is employed to test the theories in question. Respondents are divided by sex and a comparison is made between their answers to questions about the national economy, personal finances, government responsibility, abortion, ideology and party identification.

They first consider the notion that men and women might have 'systematically distinct political preferences' (Chaney, Alvarez and Nagler 1998: 313). Chaney et al.'s analysis of survey data suggests that such preferences may exist but that they are subtle and certainly not dichotomous. Chaney et al. suggest that one of the key determinates of the gender gap in voting behaviour is the difference in men's and women's perception of economic issues. Women, they propose, are most interested in the national economic situation, whilst men are more concerned with their personal economic circumstances (Chaney, Alvarez and Nagler 1998: 318). In 1992 68 per cent of the male respondents thought that the national economy was getting worse in comparison to 77 per cent of the women, indicating that women were, indeed, more pessimistic about the economy than men.

Chaney et al. test three causal relationships. The first relates to Gilligan's 'ethics of care' and suggests that women might support active government because of compassionate motivations. The second possible explanation approximates to rational choice theory. It suggests that women might support a large government 'safety net' because they are the chief consumers of public services; in this case the gender gap is believed to be self-interest motivated. The final theory that Chaney *et al*. test is that the gender gap is the result of partisan identification. Daniel Wirls argues that the gender gap is a result of a shift of men from the Democratic to Republican party rather than the result of changing patterns of behaviour among women (Wirls 1986). Wirls attributes the gender gap to women's slower rate of defection; thus emphasising partisan identification.[2] The centrality of partisan identification as an explanation of the gender gap was tested by Chaney *et al*., whose study found that there was no significant gender gap in partisan identification between 1980 and 1992, thus undermining Wirls' argument.

Chaney *et al*. employed measures of whether respondents had a positive or negative perception of the future for the national economy or their personal finances. The responses were analysed by vote and sex. The analysis was designed to test the rational choice and compassionate hypotheses. Chaney *et al*. conclude that the gender gap can be explained with an amalgamation of the theories tested. They suggest that women's less secure position within the economy combines with their compassion and motivates them to vote Democrat. They claim that the only significant issue which men and women politicise differently is the economy, and not more commonly cited 'women's issues'.

Chaney *et al*. offer an intricate explanation of the gender gap. Their work however might be enhanced by a more thorough analysis of the sub-groups of men and women involved. Many of the tables they present simply list men and women's aggregate preferences, without breaking the information down further. The lack of sub-group analysis leads us to ask why the gender gap isn't bigger. Chaney *et al*. identify many important influences that might provoke women to vote Democrat without providing explanations for the many women who in fact vote Republican. In the absence of sub-group analysis the southern religious women who vote Republican are not identified.

Jeff Manza and Clem Brooks undertook a particularly useful study of the gender gap in the United States that addresses concerns that have been omitted by other studies and which might be applied to the analysis of gender and voting behaviour in Britain (Manza and Brooks 1998). Manza and Brooks attempt to locate the origins of the gender gap by assessing National Election Study (NES) data from the eleven presidential elections from 1952 to 1992. It is their contention that other researchers have located the first gender gap in 1980 without thorough investigation. They undertake a comprehensive analysis of four models, which have been used to explain the gender gap in American voting behaviour. A detailed account of their research is useful because it can be used to hypothesise about potential gender differences in Britain.

The first model relates to the different processes of socialisation experienced by men and women. Manza and Brooks cite Carol Gilligan and Nancy Chodorow as feminists who believe that the gender gap has its foundations in childhood experiences (Chodorow 1978; Gilligan 1982). They also cite Virginia Sapiro and Sara Ruddick as feminists who support a theory linking adult socialisation to the gender gap (Ruddick 1989; Sapiro 1983). As previously outlined, these feminists claim that the different experiences of men and women, especially motherhood, shape their political preferences (Manza and Brooks 1998: 1240). Manza and Brooks state that if this model has explanatory power then the addition of 'variables representing socio-demographic cleavages' (Manza and Brooks 1998: 1244) into regression models will not account for the gender gap. For example, if the compassion thesis or the 'ethics of care' account are accurate then, even after class, education and income have been controlled for, a gender gap in voting behaviour would persist.

The second model outlined by Manza and Brooks relates to the increased autonomy possessed by women and is linked to changing marital patterns (Manza and Brooks 1998: 1239). Feminist theorists have outlined the impact of marriage on women. Heidi Hartmann claims that women's interests are subordinated by marriage and Susan Carroll suggests that a husband and wife may have shared interests that outweigh their political differences (Carroll 1988; Hartmann 1989). Should either of these contentions be true, it would be logical that a decline in the instance of the traditional family may translate into changes in voting behaviour. Manza and Brooks cite Kathleen Frankovic, who found that the sex difference in support for Reagan was at its minimum in two-adult, one-male, one-female, households (Frankovic 1982). Manza and Brooks use NES survey data to test the effects of being married on voting behaviour over forty years.

The third causal thesis is based in feminist consciousness. Manza and Brooks cite researchers such as Pamela Conover, who claim that the second wave of the women's movement resulted in a heightened feminist consciousness that translated into the gender gap (Conover 1988). They attempt to test Conover's claim using questions available in the NES data.

The final causal thesis is based in women's increased labour-force participation. Seymour Lipset proposes that exposure to political discussion in the workplace can affect policy and candidate preferences (Lipset 1960). Many researchers have attributed the reversal of the turnout gap, where more women now vote than men, to the increasing proportion of women at work and in higher education (Manza and Brookes 1998: 1242; Baxter and Lansing 1983; Clark and Clark 1986; Welch 1977). This model is particularly convincing to Manza and Brooks. They list a number of reasons why women's increased participation in the workplace might lead to a gender gap in voting behaviour. These include workplace experiences, which call into question traditional gender roles, higher dependency on public-sector employment and subsidies for families and childcare. 'The labor force participation thesis predicts that women in the workforce are the most likely to be Democratic and that the gender gap in electoral politics reflects the increasing proportion of working women' (Manza and Brooks 1998: 1244).

Using sex as a dichotomous variable, Manza and Brooks attempt to design a model to provide the best explanation for the dependent variable, the gender gap in presidential elections or the average difference in men's and women's major party vote choice. The results of their analysis lead them to conclude that the 'significant changes in the economic status of women in American society since World War I...appear to have important repercussions for electoral politics' (Manza and Brooks 1998: 1259). They claim that the increased number of women in the workforce, in conjunction with women's views on social provision and, more recently, views on the women's movement have combined to cause the gender gap. They assert that this is not the result of a socialisation process 'that all women experience, but later life experiences linked to work situation that has significant partisan effects' (Manza and Brooks 1998: 1259). They claim that the changes in the traditional family have had effects on the voting preferences of men and women and cannot therefore explain the gender gap. They also contend that, until 1992, feminist consciousness had a similar effect on men and women, with both men and women seeing the women's movement in a more favourable light. However, from the 1992 election, men and women's views about the women's movement diverged and came to have significant effects on the gender gap. Manza and Brooks outline two models of causation as illustrated below.

Figure 1.1

Primacy of social and economic change:

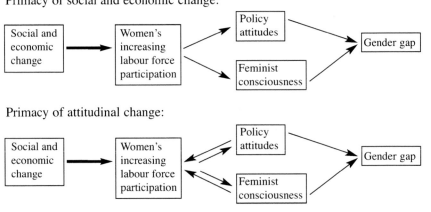

Primacy of attitudinal change:

Manza and Brooks recognise that either model could provide the best explanation of the gender gap. They assert that the models cannot be compared without survey and panel testing. The researchers' use of these two models demonstrates their sophisticated understanding of the complex arena of gender. They appreciate that gendered differences may be rooted in dual and sometimes conflicting bases. However the use of sex as a simple dichotomous variable without further sub-sector investigation may obscure other causes of the gender gap. The experiences of the socialisation of the sexes may interact with other demographic factors that could result in preferences, which are differentiated between men and women in sub-sectors, but not representative of women and men as a whole. In this research Manza and Brooks control for age, race, years of education and region (Manza and Brooks 1998: 1246). It may be however that each of these sub-groups contain a micro gender gap that could be highly relevant to understanding the nature of the gender gap as a whole. In Manza and Brook's analysis, increased labour participation appears to be the key to the gender gap in voting behaviour. However, studies that employ a more complex concept of gender tend to find a more diverse and shifting explanation more in keeping with the second model outlined above. In the light of studies that examine the gender gap with in sub-sectors, such as age cohorts, race, religion and education, Manza and Brooks' conclusion, that the explanation for the gender gap is increased 'labour force' participation needs further exploration. They outline the conflicting theoretical explanations with consistent rigour but they do not extend their research design to include a thorough analysis of the effect of sex within sub-sectors. The recognition of the complex interaction of sex with other variables would permit a more rigorous analysis of the theories they mention. It might be that the compassion thesis is most applicable to secular educated women or that religion has a strong effect on the vote choice of Southern women; but these potential differences are obscured by aggregate-level analysis. The gender gap in voting is only a marginal percentage point difference but it might underlie more profound differences within sub-groups. An understanding of how sex differences are constructed within sub-groups will provide models that can predict and explain gender gaps and how they shift and change over time.

Kristi Andersen advocates an approach to the gender gap that includes sub-groups of women (Andersen 1999). 'Ideally, one would want to develop a theoretical approach to explaining the "gender gap" that could help us understand its attitudinal and experiential sources, its variation among groups (racial, age, educational, and so forth), and its variation over time' (Andersen 1999: 17). She analyses NES data and tests theories that explain the gender gap with reference to self-interest. She asserts that 8 per cent of men work in jobs close to government, in comparison to 27 per cent of women. She adds that 49 per cent of women receive government payments, in comparison to 33 per cent of men. She states that individuals who were working in jobs close to government and receiving means-tested payments had a tendency to vote for Clinton in 1996. She then contends that the gender gap had disappeared amongst those individuals whose work suggests a close connection to the welfare state. Among those receiving government payments the gender gap was halved. The logical conclusions that might be drawn from these figures are that it is women's tendency to work in the public sector and the higher probability that women will be receivers of benefits that causes the gender gap and not any innate difference between men and women. Andersen argues that assessing the gender gap in terms of issues misses why women may have these preferences (Andersen 1999: 3).

Many recent studies of gender and voting behaviour have successfully utilised a concept of gender to provide detailed understanding of the gender gap across sub-sectors. These studies are underpinned by theories, which suggest that different behaviour between men and women will be mediated by socialisation or life experience and may be differentiated across sub-sectors. Studies that fail to recognise the complex nature of gendered behaviour may fail to identify the true roots of the gender gap.

Laura and Franco Mattei apply a concept of gender to the study of voting behaviour (Mattei and Mattei 1998). They state that if 'gender applies to understanding women's political behaviour it ought to work similarly well in explaining mens" (Mattei and Mattei 1998: 415). They claim that a notion of gender requires that variables such as inequalities in the distribution of resources, education and income be included in explanatory models and argue that these variables are usually included in theories of voting behaviour but that they are rarely 'interpreted in the light of gender' (Mattei and Mattei 1998: 416). Mattei and Mattei use NES data from 1980–96 to assess whether sex might change party coalitions in the long term. They conclude that the central reason for the gender gap in voting behaviour is the defection of men from the Democrats and not the conversion of previously Republican women. They state that overall there was a 10 per cent drop in male Democratic identifiers between 1980 and 1994. They assert that 1994 was a bad year for the Democrats with regard to both sexes. They demonstrate that there was a resurgence of support among women in 1996, which was not replicated in the male population. Mattei and Mattei assert that in 1994 the whole electorate, men and women, were less disposed to support the Democrats than at any other time. Women preferred the Democrats, but by a small margin, while men preferred the Republicans by a large margin. They claim that the 'Democrats would have retained control of both the house and the senate if women had been as excited about the Democrats, as men were about the Republicans' (Mattei and Mattei 1998: 419). They explain this with reference to the difference evident in the data between the total and actual electorate.[3] In 1994, in the total electorate, women were 9.5 per cent more Democratic than men were, in the actual electorate they were 11.9 per cent more Democratic than men were. The key factor is that, in the total electorate, men were 5.4 per cent more Republican than women were, but in the actual electorate they were 11 per cent more Republican than women were. These percentages can be used to support the 'angry white male' thesis, whereby the gender gap is explained by the reactionary politics of men and not any shift in women's behaviour. Mattei and Mattei highlight a fundamental difference between the 1994, 1992 and 1996 elections. 1994 was a mid-term election and therefore turnout was significantly reduced. In 1996 being female increased the probability of being Democrat by 6 per cent, in 1994 this figure was 11 per cent. However, if the model is expanded to include all respondents and not just those who voted, the figure is halved. Thus the gender gap in mobilisation of support was most significant in 1994 rather than the overall gender gap in partisan preference.

Mattei and Mattei are careful to consider the impact of the sex variable across other statistically significant demographic variables. For example, they refer to the overall preference for the Democratic Party among African-American voters, and suggest that in this sub-sector the impact of sex on party choice will be less profound. Mattei and Mattei discuss the potential salience of the sex variables for the two main parties in American politics. They argue that because the sexes are not homogeneous groups, unlike, perhaps, racial or religious groups, sex is unlikely to become such a key predictor of electoral behaviour. However, they propose that because of the sheer size of the groups concerned, sex could have a key role to play in future party manifestos and social alignment.

Mattei and Mattei provide a detailed and insightful analysis of the 1994 election in comparison to other congressional elections, including 1996. They are careful to consider the impact of the sex variable on specific sub-sectors within the population. They state that 'sex is a much more inclusive criterion and less clearly aligned with the issues that, over the long run, have drawn the sharpest lines of distinction between the two major parties' (Mattei and Mattei 1998: 426). If interpreted from a feminist theoretical perspective this statement has interesting implications for the study of gender and voting behaviour.

The traditionally polarised and adversarial political debates evident in many western countries, especially those with a two-party, first-past-the-post system, may have excluded the voice of feminist concern. Such exclusion could have occurred through the employment of a political system that fails to recognise the nuanced nature of political opinions and their possible gendered effects. In order to have an impact, opinions and preferences must be recognised by political parties, who must be able to identify possible political gain in satisfying them. In the case of gender this representative role is not easily fulfilled. The sex variable is an inadequate representation of the diversity of gender difference. However, the sex variable is the most obvious statistic to employ when trying to answer questions about how men and women vote. It is perhaps the intricacies of why men and women prefer one party or another that are most important, rather than the aggregate analysis of something described as partisan identification. The articles reviewed below will be analysed in the light of this thought about gender and its implications for the study of voting behaviour. The approach from here therefore, is to shift the emphasis from looking at aggregate percentage-point differences to the analysis of a potential motivational gender gap.

A motivational gender gap would occur if men and women vote for the same parties for different reasons. If such a motivational gap exists then the aggregate gap will fluctuate according to the salience of issues in each election. For example, if women vote for the party they believe will provide the best social services and men vote for the party they believe will be better at running the economy, gender gaps will only occur when no single party is credited with both capacities. Understanding the motivational gender gap would provide predictive models of electoral outcomes by linking demographic factors to attitudes and finally to issue salience.

A particularly interesting study of the 1992 American presidential election was conducted by Mary Bendyna and Celinda Lake (Bendyna and Lake 1994). They found that in 1992 the turnout rate was slightly higher for women than for men and throughout the campaign women supported Bill Clinton in greater numbers than men. These factors contributed to Clinton's presidential victory in 1992. Overall, Clinton constantly won a majority of college-educated women's support. However 'born-again' southern religious women, according to Bendyna and Lake, were mainly responsible for the increase in female George Bush supporters during the Republican National Convention in mid August. In the 1992 election, Clinton won 43 per cent of the vote, Bush 38 per cent and Perot 19 per cent. Overall, 46 per cent of women voted for Clinton compared to 41 per cent of men. Ross Perot received 4 per cent more votes from men than women and there was no gender gap for Bush (Bendyna and Lake 1994).

If only the two main parties are considered then the gender gap is magnified: Clinton received 9 per cent more votes among women than did Bush, while the difference was only 3 per cent among men. Clinton did particularly well among college-educated women and women with less than a high school education. In the youngest and oldest age cohorts Clinton benefited from the voting preference of the majority of women. Among working women the preference for Clinton over Bush was 10 per cent. However, homemakers were more likely to vote for Bush; 45 per cent of homemakers voted for Bush compared to 36 per cent for Clinton. More white women voted for Clinton than white men but the majority of white women did not vote for Clinton. African-Americans were more likely to vote Democrat than Republican. There was a small gender gap in Clinton's favour among African-American women. Nationally the gender gap was relatively small, but in twenty-two states more women backed Clinton than men in double digit figures. This situation was reversed in only six states.

Bendyna and Lake assert that two issues most influenced the voting behaviour of women: the quality of the candidate and issues such as education, abortion and healthcare. Men, they claim, were more interested in the budget deficit and the economy. Women who worked outside the home were interested in how to combine work and family. Women who had had less than high school education were concerned with their own and their children's futures. It is Bendyna and Lake's contention that in 1992 women 'had an agenda and to a surprising extent agreed' (Bendyna and Lake 1994: 251). They also say that 'even when women and men arrive at the same conclusions their different perspectives and experiences influence their judgement about candidates and policies' (Bendyna and Lake 1994: 252). Bendyna and Lake emphasise the need for an adequate concept of gender when studying voting behaviour. A relatively small aggregate gender gap may hide a more complex picture, where women vote significantly differently from the men of the same sub-group. Such differences are important because at 'the margin the different choices made by men and women can affect outcomes' (Bendyna and Lake 1994: 252). An adequate concept of gender is necessary to identify trends that may be relevant to the decision-making processes of political elites and have implications for representation issues in American politics. For example, if the interests of religious and secular women differ, but also differ from religious and secular men, effective representation must recognise this.

Susan Carroll highlights some of the oversights that occur when the gender gap is analysed without reference to a well-developed theory of gender. She uses the 1996 presidential election as an example of how the media uses news frames to report on voting behaviour and how this practice can obscure genuine voting patterns, to many women's disadvantage (Carroll 1999). The media and campaigners' obsession with the so-called 'Soccer Mom' phenomenon 'deflected attention away from other sub-groups including feminists, older women, women on welfare, women of color and professional women' (Carroll 1999: 7). During the presidential campaigns Clinton did not refer directly to Soccer Moms but many of his policy statements reflected what were perceived to be their interests. Dole, however, referred to Soccer Moms on several occasions and 'began to operate as though soccer moms were a real identity group in American society' (Carroll 1999: 10). Carroll claims that the large gender gap present in the 1996 presidential election failed to translate into power for women's groups because the emphasis on the Soccer Mom made large sections of the female electorate invisible to the political parties. In reality the title Soccer Mom could be appropriately applied to fewer than 10 per cent of the voting electorate and exit polls show that their votes made no real difference to the outcome.

Although Carroll directs her analysis at media coverage of voting behaviour, it highlights some key concerns for academic research. The study of gender and voting cannot be understood simply as the difference between women and men as a whole and the gender gap ought not to be attributed to one distinct sub-group without detailed analysis of the differences between women, as well as the similarities they share.

Janet M. Box-Steffensmeir, Suzanna DeBoef and Tse-Min Lin demonstrate the possibility that competing theories of causation may reflect the motivations of different sub-groups. For example the compassion thesis might explain the gender gap within higher income groups and the self-interest/rational choice explanation might provide a more powerful explanation among lower income groups (Box-Steffensmeir, DeBoef and Lin 1997). Steffensmeir et al. compare two competing theories of causation. The first relates to Gilligan's 'ethics of care', according to which women are in general understood to perceive morality within a connected web of human relationships in contrast to the hierarchy generally conceived by men. When applied to theories of voting behaviour an approach drawing on Gilligan's work would allow women a compassionate motivation for voting for the Democrats. Such voters may believe they are part of a structure of societal care that must support the needs of all its members. Box-Steffensmeir et al.'s hypotheses are supported by the work of Susan Welch and John Hibbing, who suggest that men are more likely than women to vote with their pocket books and therefore may be inclined to identify with the Republicans (Welch and Hibbing 1992).

Box-Steffensmeir et al. compare the compassion hypothesis to one that is bounded by self-interested behaviour, an approach they contend is more common in political-science research and literature (Box-Steffensmeir, DeBoef and Lin

1997: 3). Self-interest theories locate the gender gap in the pattern of employment and welfare dependency. Women are more likely than men to work in the public sector, a factor known to be linked to identification with the Democratic Party. Women are also more likely than men to be the receivers of state benefits: again, a factor linked with support for the Democrats.

Box-Steffensmeir *et al.* also identify the economy as an important component of the gender gap. Women, they claim, are more likely to be pessimistic about the economy than men are. This means that the economic climate would be expected to affect the gender gap. In order to test the theories Box-Steffensmeir *et al.* control for personal economic conditions, claiming that, if the gap remained after controlling for personal finances, it could be inferred that the gender gap is not purely a result of women's relatively-worse-off position in society.

Box-Steffensmeir *et al.* demonstrate that 'men and women have distinct partisan preferences and that these differences have changed over time' (Box-Steffensmeir, DeBoef and Lin 1997: 14). They demonstrate that women in higher- and middle-income groups are more likely than men, of the same socio-economic status, to be motivated by compassion. A similar although smaller gap is present at lower income levels. The fundamental feature of the research design is that it contains a method that facilitates understanding the differences between women as well as their similarities. Box-Steffensmeir *et al.* demonstrate that the state of the economy may have a more direct effect on the gender gap in middle-income groups, and that the reasons that women are more inclined to identify with the Democrats are diverse. They point out the total gender gap is relatively small – 5–10 per cent – but that this is big enough to affect election outcomes. The results of their research indicate that neither the compassion nor the self-interest arguments is sufficient, alone, but can be used together to explain the gender gap.

It is relevant to review Gill Steel's research on class and gender in British elections here because it attempts to explain why a gender gap is evident in the US and not in Britain (Steel 2003). Steel uses multinomial probit analysis. She explains the absence of a gender gap in Britain to a strong class politics.

> In liberal welfare states, women are more dependent than men on the state for benefits and employment, and therefore some women are more likely than men to support parties that offer these provisions. In both the US and Britain, women earn less than men and are primary caregivers to their families. But the crucial difference is that in the US, women live and raise children under limited welfare provisions... (Steel 2003: 3).

Welfare provision is an issue which divides the sexes and Steel suggests that in the US it has a salience that is unparalleled in Britain, thus explaining the gender gap.

Steel tests for sub-group effects by employing interaction terms. Steel tests Norris's gender generation gap theory by including an interaction term for sex and cohort. Steel finds a significant gender generation gap in the 1997 British Election Study (BES). She reminds us that this might not be evidence of gender realignment but could be a temporary fluctuation. Steel also includes interaction terms for policy preferences and sex. She finds no evidence for a motivational gender gap. However, Norris's theory suggests that different variables will explain the voting preferences in different cohorts, thus traditional values might explain the votes of older women and attitudes to social services might explain the votes of younger women. Steel notes that sub-group gender gaps may cancel each other out at the aggregate level (Steel 2003: 7). In order to test for a generational motivational gender gap we would need to include further interaction terms for sex/cohort/attitude. Inclusion of such a battery of terms would not permit parsimonious modelling and may be difficult to interpret. Thus using interaction terms doesn't easily allow us to test the motivational gender gap thesis within sub-groups. An alternative to the use of interaction terms is to divide the sample into different sub-groups; this facilitates insight into the potentially gendered aspects of all of the relationships. The research presented in this book will therefore use a process whereby analysis is conducted on separate groups and then significant differences are tested on the whole sample using interaction terms. This approach avoids the problem of including a huge array of interaction terms.

Separate sample analysis was the approach used by John Scott, Richard Matland, Phillip Michelback and Brian Bornstein (Scott *et al.* 2001). Scott *et al.* conducted an experimental study of justice norms concerning income distribution. In their analysis they found an unexpected gender difference 'between how women and men use and weigh these [allocation] principles' (Scott *et al.* 2001: 749). The findings tend to support the 'ethics of care' thesis. 'Women in our study were behaving more sociotropically, reacting to the information about the degree to which merit is said to predict income in society as a whole, and men were behaving more egoistically, with their equality-efficiency preferences determined by their individual ideological beliefs' (Scott *et al.* 2001: 764). Scott *et al.*'s study is relevant to a study of gender and voting because it provides evidence that men and women might approach questions of distributive justice (and thus politics) in different ways.

After Scott *et al.* found an unexpected gender gap they 'divided the sample into women and men and reran the regressions on the separate samples…the significant effect of the merit manipulation seen in the aggregate results was driven by women…while ideology doesn't have an effect on the aggregate level, dividing the sample reveals a strong effect for men but no effect for women…men are somewhat more strongly affected by SES, with higher-SES participants more concerned with efficiency' (Scott *et al.* 2001: 757). Scott *et al.* found that relationships at the aggregate level were masking gender effects. Thus although ideology appeared to have no effect on the whole sample it did have an effect on the choices of men. Scott *et al.*'s research demonstrates that when examining gender effects it is beneficial to examine separate samples. In this research indirect relationships will be assessed by analysing variables according to their causal order and by conducting research on separate samples of men and women (and men and women from different birth cohorts).

The final study of gender and voting behaviour to be reviewed in this section is Pippa Norris and Ronald Inglehart's global gender generation gap (Inglehart and Norris 2000). Inglehart and Norris are reviewed here because their work covers both the US and British context. They extend Norris's gender generation gap theory, which focused mainly on Britain, to a global context (Norris 1999). Norris outlines competing explanations of the gender gap. The first explanation is the traditional perspective whereby women are considered to be more likely to vote for the Conservative Party than men, exemplified by the writing of Campbell *et al.* (Campbell *et al.* 1960). The second explanation is the convergence thesis. This theory suggests that as women and men's lifestyles approximate each other more closely their voting patterns will merge. The final explanation is the revisionist perspective, which claims that the previous gender difference in voting may have reversed. Inglehart and Norris are proponents of the revisionist perspective. They state that younger women in western democracies are more 'left leaning' than older women who still conform to the notion of the female Conservative voter.

Elsewhere, Norris demonstrates how an analysis of gender and voting behaviour for the 1997 British general election leads to the rejection of both the traditional and revisionist hypothesis if sex is employed as a dichotomous variable (Norris 1999). However, if the population is divided into age cohorts the conclusions she reaches are different. In 1997 55 per cent of young women under forty-five voted Labour, in comparison to only 44 per cent of younger men. In the older age group (over forty-four) 39 per cent of the women voted Conservative in comparison to 31 per cent of the older men.

Inglehart and Norris then extend their analysis to consider the possibility of a gender-generation gap internationally. They provide an interesting argument in support of this thesis. The key point is that what can look like sufficient evidence to undermine a theory needs to be tested and retested in the context of gender. This is because the sex variable interacts with a diverse and sometimes conflicting range of other variables and is no sense geographically located; its implications are therefore constantly shifting in conjunction with other political realignments.

The US gender gap research offers a useful tool to add to the analysis of British voting behaviour because it provides examples of good practice alongside possible hypotheses. The review has highlighted the importance of considering sub-group differences in order to employ a concept of gender. There is a need for a comprehensive consideration of the difference between sex and gender at the planning stage of any analysis of gender and voting behaviour. This difference must be clear throughout the research design and considered during the research process, or the project will be fundamentally weakened. In this research, the sub-group analysis will concentrate on comparing men and women from different generations.

## BEYOND THE GENDER GAP?

There has been some criticism of the use of the term gender gap in the US. Researchers are accused of using the gender gap to further a political agenda (Greenberg 2001; Seltzer, Newman and Leighton 1997; Steel 2003). The approach adopted here attempts to redress these criticisms by looking beyond the gender gap, conceiving gendered behaviours and/or attitudes as tectonic plates that may shift and reveal hidden effects. More simply, the research conducted here will test the possibility that men and women (and men and women from different sub-groups) may vote for the same parties for different reasons or that motivational gender gaps might exist.

Seltzer *et al.* compile a list of ten myths about women and politics (Seltzer, Newman and Leighton 1997). Amongst these is a reminder that the gender gap in the United States is not a chasm. They highlight that there are much larger gaps between other sub-groups. For example 'in 1994, women voted seven to eleven percentage points more Democratic than men...and the race gap between whites and blacks was a true chasm of 50 points' (Seltzer, Newman, and Leighton 1997: 3).

Norris highlights how the term 'gender gap' has been utilised in the United States, both by the women's movement to pursue their agenda and by the media as a convenient peg on which to hang election reporting (Norris 2001). The political nature of the term 'gender gap' was also criticised by Kaufmann and Petrocik. They claimed that, contrary to other approaches, the gender gap in the United States could be accounted for by the changing partisanship of American men (Kaufmann and Petrocik 1999).

Anna Greenberg claims that after the 1996 presidential election there was a tendency for commentators and activists to describe the Democrat vote as the women's vote (Greenberg 2001). However, Greenberg notes that white women did not tend to vote Democrat and in fact 54 per cent of white women voted Republican. 'Important sectors of the female electorate have political concerns that are at odds with the Democrat Party, though they hold these preferences less strongly than men do' (Greenberg 2001: 2).

As well as considering aggregate and sub-group gender gaps in voting this research will consider motivational gender gaps. Gill Steel used the term motivational gender gap to describe a situation where men and women might vote for the same party for different reasons (Steel 2003). Such an approach can help us to avoid using the term 'gender gap' in a political way whilst simultaneously avoiding the analysis of small percentage point differences.


## HYPOTHESIS GENERATION

Chapters three to seven contain the data analysis performed in this study. However, the chapters are linked steps and together attempt to answer the same overarching questions. It is, therefore, helpful to outline the central themes to be addressed and the hypotheses to be tested.

The core question of the research is 'in what way and to what extent are women's political preferences different to men's, as expressed in voting behaviour?'

This core question is operationalised by utilising the terminology and findings of research pertaining to the phenomenon labelled the 'gender gap' in the United States and the less substantial body of research conducted into gender and voting behaviour in Britain. The central questions generated in this way are:

1) Why gender dealignment in Britain?
2) Is there evidence to support Norris's gender generation gap theory?
3) If left-leaning political parties provide women-friendly platforms, is a modern gender gap likely to emerge in Britain to match the one currently evident in the United States?

As discussed previously Pippa Norris has summarised the distinct periods apparent in the relationship between sex and vote at the aggregate level in the US and Great Britain (Norris 1999). The first period encompasses the 1960s and 1970s, and possibly earlier (Tingsten 1937). In this epoch the traditional gender gap was apparent, in the United States, Western Europe and Britain. In these countries women were slightly more likely than men to support parties on the centre right, a pattern highlighted by contemporary political scientists (Butler and Stokes 1974; Campbell *et al.* 1960; Duverger 1955). The traditional pattern was replaced in the 1980s by a phenomenon Norris terms gender dealignment, where any sex differences in vote at the aggregate level were insignificant (Hayes 1997; Heath, Jowell and Curtice 1985; Rose and McAllister 1986), Norris describes the final phase of gender and vote as gender realignment. Gender realignment began in the United States when in the 1980 presidential election more women than men voted for the Democratic candidate. Since then, in most national and all presidential elections more women have voted for the Democratic candidate than men, and more men have voted for the Republican candidate than women. Inglehart and Norris found evidence of the modern gender gap in the 1990s in several other advanced industrialised nations: Japan, Ireland, Denmark, Austria, the Netherlands, Norway, Sweden, Switzerland and Canada (Inglehart and Norris 2000). There was not a significant difference between the vote choices of the sexes in West Germany, Italy, Northern Ireland, Portugal, Iceland, Britain, Australia, France, Hungary and Belgium (Inglehart and Norris 2000). However, Inglehart and Norris also calculated an ideology gap for a number of countries for 1981 and 1990.[4] The reported ideology gaps for 1981 are –0.03 for the US and –0.06 for Britain. The gap reported for 1990 was 0.22 for the US and 0.19 for Britain. Thus the trend evident in ideology in the US, with women becoming more left-leaning than men, was also evident in Britain but was translated into an aggregate level gender gap in voting in the US and not in Britain. Inglehart and Norris took their data from the World Values Survey (WVS), in which ideology was measured by self-placement on a 10-point, left-right scale. There is no reason to assume that WVS would be an unreliable measure for US/British comparison. However, it would be reinforced or tested by an evaluation of trends in summed scales. The similarity in the gender gap in ideology between the US and Britain is enough in itself to warrant a thorough examination of the relationship between gender, ideology and vote in Britain.

## US versus Britain: Possible sources of difference

Norris presents several factors that might account for the modern gender gap within the United States. 'The traditional lack of a strong class cleavage in the electorate, the centrist pattern of two-party competition, or the salience of issues like abortion and affirmative action' (Norris 2001: 302). If these differences account for the gender gap in vote in the United States then there are three possible outcomes for the British context. Firstly, there might be no relationship between gender and ideology and gender and vote in the Britain, because the gender gap in the United States is a national phenomenon. Secondly, there could be a relationship between gender and ideology that does not translate into vote in Britain, because the ideological underpinnings of the gender gap might not map on to salient electoral issues or they might only be relevant within specific sub-groups. Alternatively, the specifics of the electoral context in Britain may produce gendered voting patterns that are different to those found in the United States. American women have historically had greater access to higher education than women in many other western industrial nations (Jennings and Farah 1980). Hence it is worth exploring the relationship between education, sex, ideology and vote in Britain.

Another area of difference between the United States and Britain is that of attitudes to race and race relations. Warren Miller and Merrill Shanks suggest that the gender gap in the United States might be accounted for by Southern white men switching their partisanship from the Democrats to the Republicans (Miller and Shanks 1996). The suggestion that the gender gap can be attributed to the changing patterns of men, has also been supported by Wirls (Wirls 1986).

In Britain, the 1950s and 1960s are sometimes referred to as the era of consensus politics. Unlike the US at this time, the key differences between the two main parties in Britain centred around the issue of nationalisation/denationalisation/renationalisation. It is possible that men's and women's attitudes to health and education were different in the 1950s and 60s, but this attitudinal difference might not have translated into a gender gap in vote, because the two main parties were not offering substantially different platforms on health and education issues. Chapter three will assess whether there were ideological or issue preference differences between the sexes. Chapters four to seven will focus on the relationship between issue preference and vote, or issue salience.

The relevance of issue salience to studies of gender and vote was highlighted by Karen Kaufmann and John Petrocik (Kaufmann and Petrocik 1999). In their discussion of the gender gap in vote and partisan identification in the United States they found that,

Men were more conservative than women on social welfare questions during the entire 1952–1996 period. But their party preference began to conform to their social welfare attitudes between 1966 and 1978, when party disputes about 'big government' and welfare spending became more salient with the arrival of militant Republicanism in the form of Goldwater and later Ronald Reagan (Kaufmann and Petrocik 1999: 883).

However, if this is an explanation for the emergence of the modern gender gap in the United States, should not the arrival of the Thatcher government have polarised the debate in Britain in the same way? It is possible that the strength of the relationship between class and vote in Britain prevented such a gender gap emerging. Alternatively the absence of an aggregate-level gender gap may be the result of the Labour Party being less attractive to women than the Democrats in the United States. The Labour Party may have been perceived as overtly masculine. Alternatively, the issue agenda that Labour was promoting might not have appealed to the women who shared characteristics with the women who voted Democrat in the United States.

Feminist theories of the modern gender gap in the US often claim that women are more concerned than men about welfare provision. Although this might be understood to be a left-leaning attribute it may well not be a covariant of attitudes to nationalisation. Did the forces that caused a gender gap in the US, with more women supporting the Democrats, lead to a split vote amongst similar women in the UK between the Labour Party and the Liberals (SDP, Liberal Democrats)? There is no suggestion here that self-identified socialist women would not prioritise nationalisation, but gender gap theories emerging from the United States do not engage with the historically class-based politics of Britain, and the salience of nationalisation. Feminist philosophy suggests that women's left-leaning inclinations should be based in an altruistic concern for the poor and needy, as well as support for state funded health and education provision. If British parties are divided by class-based issues we might, therefore, not expect a gender gap to emerge.

It is possible that men and women may have different motivations for choosing between the Labour Party and the Liberal Democrats. In their analysis of the 1983 British Election Study, Evans et al. find that attitudes to nationalisation successfully distinguish between Labour supporters and Liberal supporters (Evans, Heath and Lalljee 1996). They found that Liberal and Labour supporters did not have significantly different locations on the visual left-right scale, the libertarian-authoritarian scale or the postmaterialism index but that Liberal supporters were further right on the left-right scale than Labour supporters and they were less likely to support nationalisation. If nationalisation is not a key feature of the left-leaning inclinations of younger women they might be more inclined to support the Liberal Democrats than men. However, since the Labour party has modernised and dropped Clause Four it may have become more appealing to younger women, thus creating a gender generation gap. In addition, the Labour campaigns in 1997 and 2001 repeatedly emphasised hospitals and schools and in this respect may have appealed to women voters. Therefore, the research presented in Chapters three to seven will consider whether women are more likely to vote for the Liberal Democrats than men.

## SUMMARY

This chapter has outlined the theoretical and empirical reasons for studying gender and vote in Britain. Feminist approaches to theory and method have been outlined, discussed and use for hypothesis generation. The chapter has also summarised the US gender-gap literature to develop hypotheses to test in the British case. Furthermore, the review was used to develop an approach to the study of gender and vote that looks beyond the gender gap to sub-group differences.

## NOTES

1   Women are better represented in British devolved institutions. Following the 1999 election women constituted 37.2 per cent of members of the Scottish Parliament and after the 2000 election 41.7 per cent of the AMs returned to the Welsh Assembly were women (Squires and Wickham-Jones 2001). It should be noted that the higher proportions of female representatives evident in the devolved assemblies can be largely attributed to equality promoting measures, such as twinning seats and zipping lists, employed by political parties.

2   Partisan identification is a difficult variable to control for because it is relevant to many other causal variables, such as leadership and party evaluations, and may vary by election.

3   The term 'total electorate' refers to those who were registered to vote; the 'actual electorate' is those voters who turned out.

4   The ideology gap is measured as the difference between the mean position of women and men on the 10-point, left-right ideology scale. A negative figure indicates women are more rightwing than men. A positive figure indicates women are more leftwing than men.

# chapter two | mainstream studies of voting behaviour

This chapter introduces and analyses mainstream voting behaviour studies. The studies are reviewed in a roughly chronological order, which is over-ridden when authors share perspectives. The earlier studies are referred to as belonging to the traditional voting behaviour literature. There was a tendency for these early studies to do away with the tenets of good science when studying the sex variable (Goot and Reid 1975). Contemporary studies are generally more sensitive to issues of gender. However, the early agenda-setting studies have, to a large extent, framed the debate with which analyses of voting are concerned and therefore gender differences are sometimes overlooked.

This chapter is intended to provide a historiography of voting behaviour studies and their analysis of sex and gender. The emphasis is on the early opinion-forming studies. The story of the study of gender and voting in Britain moves from sexist assumptions, to benign neglect to feminist studies. However, there is something of a divide in contemporary research between feminist and mainstream research. In general, mainstream studies do not focus much analysis on gender and instead usually include the sex variable as a control. Overall there is more similarity than difference in the way men and women vote and it is not surprising that the study of voting behaviour has not focused on sex differences. However, it is surprising that, prior to the 1990s, there was virtually no analysis of gender and voting behaviour. This chapter will trace the story of the evolution of electoral studies and attempt to find out why gender differences weren't explored more rigorously.

A qualification should be added that the research extensively reviewed in this chapter contains analysis of sex differences. There is a wealth of early opinion-forming research that does not consider the impact of sex on vote. These studies are mentioned briefly but the bulk of the critique is directed at the research that did mention sex differences, simply because there is more to say about them. Almond and Verba's *The Civic Culture* contains a wealth of analysis of sex difference and is an invaluable source for understanding and summarising the treatment of the sex variable during the discipline's infancy. Whilst Almond and Verba's analysis is subject to some considerable criticism in this chapter, their interest in sex differences was notable.

The reviews presented in this chapter illustrate that sex, and other factors, has tended to be overlooked because the central concern of the discipline has tended to be the impact of class on vote. Additionally, without knowledge of feminist theory it is easy to miss gender differences in political behaviour because the interaction of sex with other factors tends to produce indirect, rather than direct effects that are not always apparent at the aggregate level. Contemporary studies that are relevant to the research question will be introduced alongside the analysis in Chapters three to seven. A number of key areas of research are not reviewed extensively here, for example, studies of regional electoral patterns and swing. Other areas, such as economic voting, are introduced alongside the data analysis in Chapters three to seven.

The review starts with opinion-forming research such as that of Campbell *et al.* in *The American Voter*. The review then moves to consider British literature central to the alignment/dealignment debate. The alignment/dealignment debate is concerned with whether class remains the most dominant social cleavage and best predictor of partisan identification and thus voting behaviour. Theories that emphasise the role of class in shaping voting preference tend to provide a social/psychological account of how stable predispositions to one party are formed.

There are two fundamental tendencies generally found in the traditional voting-behaviour literature, which serve to obscure gender issues from the analytic framework. Both of these tendencies stem from the failure to subject assumptions to rigorous testing. Susan Bourque and Jeans Grossholtz criticised early 'malestream' political science research for practising bad science when analysing gender differences (Bourque and Grossholtz 1974). They assert that 'if political scientists subjected their data to more searching analysis they may have avoided assumptions used as explanation' (Bourque and Grossholtz 1974: 89).

Early studies of voting behaviour concentrated primary research on aggregate data. In general, analysing aggregate data is not problematic and is the most logical way to commence a research project. However, a problem emerges when the researcher begins to look at sub-sectors or disaggregated data, without theorising how they might be different from the population as a whole. The problem with this approach is that it is conceivable that sub-sector differences could cancel each other out at an aggregate level and therefore be undetected without further scrutiny of the data. Pippa Norris, for example, discovered a gender generation gap, whereby older women were more likely to vote Conservative than older men but younger women were more likely to vote Labour than younger men; yet no gap was evident at the aggregate level. Therefore it cannot be assumed that the lead variable at aggregate level will continue to be the most significant within sub-sectors. The researcher must develop reasonable hypotheses and alternative hypotheses relating to sub-sector interactions in order to examine the data. For example, social class might be the most significant variable at the aggregate level but, when different ethnic groups are examined, religion might be the key variable explaining issue preference or vote. Although this point might seem pedantic, dealing with a difficult variable like sex demands clear hypotheses. Sex cross-cuts and interacts with all other crucial demographic factors. Developing analytic tools that are subtle and refined enough to avoid making essentialising claims is of paramount importance.

The second but related tendency is also associated with inadequate theoretical frameworks. The theoretical statements made with regard to gender by researchers within the traditional voting behaviour school were not usually presented in the form of testable claims made prior to analysis. Instead, after the data had been presented, claims were often made on the basis of unsubstantiated assumptions. For example, gender differences were frequently attributed to an assumed link between women and family. This elision between woman and family is common in the traditional literature and is not usually accompanied by any theoretical justification. The problem is that the differences in the lives of men and women could impact on political behaviour but the traditional literature tends to treat this as static and inevitable, and perhaps natural, without any theoretical basis.

In order to trace these two key themes through the traditional voting behaviour literature, it is useful to analyse them in roughly chronological order. The order is not perfectly chronological because in some cases it makes more logical sense to consider books on common themes, often addressed to each other, together. The most coherent way to try to understand the manner in which these texts have dealt with, or ignored, gender issues is to summarise and examine the main issues with which they are concerned and to attempt to ascertain why they came to dominate the field.

## THE 'MICHIGAN MODEL': THE AMERICAN VOTER

Research into voting behaviour in the United States has had a profound effect on the direction of research in Britain. Although there was some significant research in the US prior to the 1950s, it was the work of Campbell et al. that had the most fundamental effect on the study of voting behaviour in Britain (Campbell et al. 1960). The model they developed is known as the 'Michigan' model. It was designed to contrast with the previously dominant approach advocated by Berelson et al. (Berelson et al. 1954), which can be loosely described as social determinism (Denver and Hands 1992).

The Michigan model included social influences but linked them to a psychological account of how voters develop a sense of party identification and how this is mediated through short-term factors. Campbell et al. believed that their model demonstrated the mechanisms by which political change occurred within the electorate. Societal and structural changes would have a gradual effect on levels of party support because individuals made their vote choice through a combination of a sense of party identification, considered to be a long-term factor, and short-term influences. The role of short-term influences was perceived to be minimal because most individuals appeared to vote in line with their party identification. This approach plays down the role of short-term factors because individuals were believed, in general, to be incapable of making an election-by-election choice due to their not having the tools necessary to evaluate the wealth of information available to them. Information would be filtered through a psychological framework that gave precedence to issues perceived to be important to the individual because they were of the type that were discussed around them in their community. It was in this way that Campbell *et al.* explained the influence of societal characteristics. When considering the impact that the American literature had on the British it is helpful to consider how analysis of sex was integrated into the models developed by Campbell *et al.*

In *The American Voter*, Campbell *et al.* present their evidence in support of the Michigan model. They include a brief analysis of sex and voting behaviour. They justify brevity by referring to the relatively recent event of the enfranchisement of women. With reference to women's suffrage they state that 'sufficient time has passed to invite evaluation of its consequences' (Campbell *et al.* 1960: 225). These statements indicate that sex itself was not considered interesting per se but that historic political events ensured that it merited some consideration. Their approach does not start with any theoretical explanation for differences between the political interests of men and women. In this sense it does not seek to address the sex variable in a similar way to class, regional or perhaps religious factors; these factors were embedded within a thoroughly developed theoretical and analytic framework. Campbell *et al.* concentrate their analysis of gender upon participation, specifically voter turnout. They claim that traditionally held views are 'not rapidly uprooted' (Campbell *et al.* 1960: 226) and use the tendency of some of their female interviewees to defer to their husbands, on political matters, as an illustration of this. After controlling for education Campbell *et al.* discovered that the turnout rate amongst women rose more steeply in relation to an educational scale than for men. Interestingly, they show that the difference in turnout between women with lower and higher levels of education is more pronounced than the same differences between men.

The gender gap is at its largest at the lowest educational levels. They assert that there is no evidence that men and women differ in levels of party loyalty or citizen duty. They do, however, contend that men seem to possess higher levels of self-confidence about their own abilities to understand and affect, via political participation, complex political issues. Campbell *et al.* explain this difference by hypothesising that sex roles affect the belief systems of individuals and tend to pressure women to adopt submissive roles, and vice versa, with regard to men. They also suggest that 'the ten per cent difference in vote turnout is misleading because women feel a duty to vote but defer to their husbands at other levels' (Campbell *et al.* 1960: 260) implying that the turnout gap is probably smaller than other gender gaps in participation. Campbell *et al.* say that 'if a large variety of other social characteristics are taken into account, there is no residual difference in partisanship between men and women' (Campbell *et al.* 1960: 260). The two statements indicate the tendency of Campbell *et al.* to make conclusions about sex on the basis of untested assumptions and their failure to understand sex as a cross-cutting social variable. For example, they do not test their assumption that women defer to men at other levels and they do not consider other possible reasons for the lower levels of political efficacy reported by women. One such reason might be a sense of alienation from the political system, caused by under representation. They also fail to consider the fact that women's location within specific societal groups might be more than incidental and a key feature of their voting behaviour, for example, women tend to have lower socio-economic status than men. Single mothers might not seem to have specific voting interests when social class is controlled for but their reasons for voting with the general population of their social class might be very different from the perceived norm. The treatment of the sex variable adopted by Campbell *et al.* is a precedent for a pattern of oversight and assumption continued by their critics and proponents. Campbell *et al.* were by no means the first political scientists to make unsubstantiated claims about women; however, it was their particular emphasis on socio-economic class and absence of thorough gender analysis that set the parameters of the debate about voting behaviour.

## ALMOND AND VERBA AND *THE CIVIC CULTURE*

*The Civic Culture* was first published in 1963. It was a groundbreaking text in its time and continues to be reflected upon in current literature (Almond and Verba 1963). Unlike *The American Voter*, *The Civic Culture* is not specifically located within the traditional voting behaviour literature. However, there is an overlap with that literature and political attitudes and participation are analysed in detail. Unlike most early researchers, Almond and Verba extensively research sex differences. An analysis of their research is, therefore, particularly helpful because it provides insight into the conceptualisation of sex differences in early opinion-forming studies.

The focus of *The Civic Culture* was political stability and democracy, a common post-Second-World-War theme. At this time many researchers and theorists were concerned with establishing the components of democracy and the specific variations between the warring nations. Almond and Verba developed a model which suggested that formal democratic political structures were not, in themselves, a sufficient guarantor of the political system. They suggested that there might be an interaction between political culture and political system, which can be congruent or non-congruent. When the two are not congruent, political instability occurs. In order to test their hypothesis about the relationship between political institutions, structure and culture, Almond and Verba conducted a study of electoral opinion. Their work may be read as a broad interpretation of voting behaviour and its causes.

Almond and Verba described the civic culture as a combination of modern and traditional values. In their analysis, a civic culture contains a ratio of individuals with different political perspectives. The right ratio and political structure would ensure stability. The perspectives ranged from parochial, those who dwelt on local concerns, to subject, those who felt deference towards their leaders, and finally to participant, those who felt a duty and ability to take an active political role. They claimed that a civic culture is a participant political culture when the political culture and structure are democratic and congruent, containing democratic institutions and above-threshold ratio of citizens with participant psychological perspectives. The key to a participant culture was that a reasonable number of the citizens should be able to perceive themselves as political agents.[1]

Throughout *The Civic Culture*, the male-dominated nature of politics in the countries analysed is not highlighted. The key statements made by Almond and Verba are all examined below. What is striking to the feminist reader is the absence of any plausible explanations for the gender gaps found in all the countries examined and the neglect of the whole realm of women's disenfranchisement.

The first mention of sex in *The Civic Culture* occurs on page 173 and is presented in the form of a table. The table is an analysis of citizen competence and subject competence. Competent citizens are those who believe that they are able to affect government decisions through political influence. Competent subjects are defined as those who believe that they are able to appeal to a set of regular and orderly rules in their dealings with administrative officials (Almond and Verba 1963: 177). They suggest that there are similar patterns between men and women but that the differences between the sexes with regard to administrative competence are smaller. They claim that this is an indication that political competence develops after administrative competence. However, Almond and Verba do not test this claim or develop any alternative hypothesises to rival it. For example, they do not consider that women who wished to challenge a governmental decision, at that time, would almost certainly have had to appeal to men, who may have been prejudiced against them. Instead of locating the inadequacy in the political system, women were implicitly implicated as citizens who had not achieved the same level of development as men.

The second mention of sex is on page 324, where Almond and Verba allocate a section of a chapter to 'women and political orientation'. They claim that, the advocates of women's suffrage made exaggerated claims. These included 'the abolition of poverty, protection of family life, and raising educational and cultural standards' (Almond and Verba 1963: 325) as well as zero toleration for war. It was Almond and Verba's contention that none of these things came into fruition and that 'it would appear that women differ from men in their political behaviour only in being somewhat more frequently apathetic, parochial, conservative, and sensitive to personality, emotional, and aesthetic aspects of political life and electoral campaigns' (Almond and Verba 1963: 325). A modern reader might hope that claims made in such a forthright and derogatory manner might be sufficiently supported by evidence and theory. This was largely not the case.

Within the section 'women and political orientation' Almond and Verba present a number of tables providing data by which they compare the orientations of men and women and the differences in these gender gaps between countries. The tables, however, are not clearly presented and the argument is based on unsubstantiated assumptions. The first such table refers to outgoing leisure activities

Table XII.1: Percentage who choose outgoing leisure activities; by nation and sex[2]

| Nation | Male | | Female | | Total | | |
|---|---|---|---|---|---|---|---|
| | % | n | % | n | % | n | Gender gap |
| United States | 24 | 455 | 54 | 515 | 40 | 970 | +30 |
| Great Britain | 22 | 460 | 37 | 503 | 30 | 963 | +15 |
| Germany | 18 | 449 | 13 | 506 | 16 | 955 | -5 |
| Italy | 6 | 471 | 9 | 524 | 7 | 995 | +3 |
| Mexico | 8 | 355 | 13 | 652 | 11 | 1007 | +5 |

(The gender gap figure is calculated by subtracting the male percentage from the female, country by country. The mean gender gap is +9.6 per cent)

(Almond and Verba 1963: 326).

Almond and Verba claim that in 'each of the countries studied, men showed higher frequencies and higher intensities than women, in practically all the indices of political orientation' (Almond and Verba 1963: 325). However, the element of their findings that is the most interesting to them is the variation between countries studied. They summarise these differences with reference to the open family (where women participate in public life) and its poor cousin, the closed family (in which women don't participate in public life). They highlight that in the United States and Britain women seem to spend more time in organised or social activities than those in Germany, Italy and Mexico. This is cited as evidence for open families in the first two countries and families of the closed variety in the other three.

In Table XII.1 the percentage of citizens who choose outgoing leisure activities are shown by nation and by sex. An interesting feature of the table is the fact that in the United States women reported this type of activity twice as often as men; in the UK a 15 per cent gap in women's favour is identified. It is also interesting that women also outnumbered men in Italy and Mexico. In Italy the male figure for outgoing activity was 6 per cent and the female 9 per cent. In Mexico the gap was +3. In fact the only country in which the gap was negative was Germany with –5. It is important to scrutinise these details carefully because of the statements Almond and Verba make with reference to Table XII.1. They claim that the findings suggest a type of family in the United States and Great Britain that is open to the community and open via both men and women. Whilst the activity levels do suggest greater public involvement in Britain and the US, the family implication is not obvious. Almond and Verba seem to be suggesting that, in the other countries investigated, women might be firmly located within the home as part of a 'closed family'. In Germany, however, the gender gap was found to be only 5 per cent and in Italy 3 per cent more women responded favourably to the survey question than men did; this figure was 5 per cent in Mexico. Almond and Verba might respond, in their own defence, with a claim that women, or women's lives, were more suited to the type of activities implied by the question. However the reader must bear in mind that when, with reference to Table XII.1,

Table XII.2: Percentage who discuss politics; by sex and education[3]

| Nation | Total | | | Primary (or less) | | | Secondary (or more) | | | Gender gap by education[5] |
|--------|-------|-----|--------|------|-----|--------|------|-----|--------|------|
| | Male | GG[4] | Female | Male | GG | Female | Male | GG | Female | |
| United States | 83% | -13 | 70% | 73% | -16 | 57% | 95% | -12 | 83% | -14 |
| Great Britain | 77% | -14 | 63% | 74% | -18 | 56% | 83% | -8 | 75% | -10 |
| Germany | 77% | -31 | 46% | 74% | -32 | 42% | 88% | -14 | 74% | -18 |
| Italy | 47% | -29 | 18% | 36% | -23 | 13% | 64% | -27 | 37% | +4 |
| Mexico | 55% | -26 | 29% | 49% | -22 | 26% | 77% | -21 | 56% | -1 |

Almond and Verba talk about 'political, community, religious and social forms of free-time activity' (Almond and Verba 1963: 325), such activities do not appear to imply location in the feminine domain. However, even if open and closed families exist, the suggestion that the data provides evidence for them is preposterous. Further investigation into exactly what type of activities the male and female respondents pursue and the differences between them is required but not offered by Almond and Verba.

Almond and Verba then turn their attention to the percentage of respondents who claim to discuss politics. They present their data by sex and by education. They find that, in each of the countries investigated, more men than women reported that they discussed politics.

The total figures show a gender gap in the US and UK of –3 per cent and –4 per cent respectively, the gap increases to 31 per cent in Germany, 29 per cent in Italy and 26 per cent in Mexico. The gender gap by education varies between 16 and 32 per cent for those with a primary education, or less. The lowest figure is found in the US, 16 per cent, followed closely by the UK with 18 per cent, Germany with 32 per cent and Italy and Mexico, 23 and 22 per cent respectively. When those with a secondary education or more are considered, the gender gap falls in every country bar Italy, although the fall is negligible in Mexico.

The weakness in Almond and Verba's analysis is that they look at the aggregate proportions and not the percentage point differences between sub-groups. The percentage point gaps are outlined above. In their analysis, Almond and Verba state that 'at the level of secondary education or higher, the proportions of women who discuss politics in the United States, Britain, and Germany reach or exceed three-quarters. The increase in Mexico is substantial; whereas in Italy, though the increase from primary to secondary is large, only a little more than one-third of the educated feminine population report that they talk politics' (Almond and Verba 1963: 327). Almond and Verba used the data in Table XII.2 to support their claim that in America and Britain there was an open family structure. They believe Germany to be more closed than the first two but less so than Mexico and Italy. Almond and Verba's emphasis on the Italian case, suggesting that the increase from primary to secondary education is large but that still too few women discuss politics at the level of secondary education, may be misleading. This is because, although more women claim to discuss politics in the latter group, the rise is in keeping with the increase in the number of men discussing politics in the equivalent group. The percentage of women who don't discuss politics does not fluctuate in relation to men; in this case education cannot be implicated as a consequential factor on the gender gap and the closed family.

In short, although Almond and Verba present tables which offer sex as a possible demographic variable they do not sufficiently utilise it. In this case they presented data on both men and women alongside aggregate data. This provided the opportunity for some interesting gendered analysis. However, because Almond and Verba were interested in the differences between countries and not the sexes, they failed to look at the gender gap country by country. If they had, they would have discovered that higher education levels reduced the gender gap in Britain, America and Germany, increased it slightly in Italy and had no effect in Mexico. It would seem that in general *The Civic Culture* either subsumes women into a gendered (masculine) citizen, or treats them as an entirely different entity interchangeable with the family. In their discussion the percentages of women are considered separately and questions are not raised as to why they illustrate patterns that differ from men's. Instead what is deemed to be of interest is the difference between women from different countries.

Almond and Verba state that at 'the level of primary education or less, the differences between the sexes are more pronounced in all five countries' (Almond and Verba 1963: 327). If this is relational to secondary education or more it is not true in the case of Italy, and tenuous in the case of Mexico. If it is related to the total figures, Germany displays negligible differences. The reason for these errors is that Almond and Verba are not genuinely interested in teasing out the influence of sex on political orientation. Their primary concern is to find some empirically testable qualities shared by Britain and America that can be strung together as a recipe for stability, of which a threshold of female participation might be considered to be an ingredient; because of this approach statements made about sex and gender are rarely scrutinised.

From their statements Almond and Verba conclude that, in the US and UK, the 'family becomes part of the system of political communications'. They state that in Italy the general rate of political discussion is low and when men talk about politics they tend to do it outside of the home. The suggestion is that the only place women might discuss politics is at home with their husbands. This seems a strong statement to direct exclusively at Italy, without further investigation. Although education appears to have little influence on the gender gap in Italy it is not obvious why the home is the trigger. It may be reasonably assumed that even the most domesticated of women had some contact with others than their husbands. Almond and Verba appear never to contemplate the fact that the male-dominated world of politics they are researching may be an inhospitable environment to women, for reasons other than their own apathy and dependence on their husbands.

After rigorous examination it is apparent that many of Almond and Verba's claims about women were not reasonably substantiated. Furthermore the assumptions which masked the gender implications from the data also prohibited a thorough investigation of what implications might actually be present.

In order to conclude their discussion of women and political orientation Almond and Verba assert that 'the significance of the political emancipation of women is not in the suffragette's dream of women in cabinets, parliaments, at the upper levels of the civil service, and the like; nor is it in Duverger's conception of the dependent minor' (*ibid*. pp. 334). Almond and Verba suggest that in America and Britain, society permits an open family which, 'enables children to develop within the family itself a sense of political competence and obligation' (*ibid*.). This seems to be the crux of their interest in women. They appear to be suggesting that women should feel subjectively competent in order to reinforce the political culture through their children. Hence, women are not important in themselves but are located in private life. Indeed, the term 'women' is frequently elided with family or private life in their analysis.

Their elision of women/family/private prevents Almond and Verba from unravelling the causes of women's disenfranchisement. Their failure leads them to the false prediction that women would not enter actively into political structures. The tendency to treat women as family has, I think, several roots. Firstly, Almond and Verba tend to consider a lack of participation as the result of women's unwillingness. Consideration is not given to possible barriers that might prevent or impede that participation. They also argue that a stable culture probably contains a mix of citizens with subject and participant orientations. Therefore, they begin their analysis with the prediction that they will find individuals who feel that they are unable to affect the political system, even within stable political systems. Evidence of such disenfranchisement may be benign if it is randomly distributed. For example, it may be an effect of a personality trait. However, when such characteristics are particularly located in specific sub-groups we need to consider if such groups are excluded, if they experience systematic barriers to participation. It was exclusion which Almond and Verba feared. When they found evidence of exclusion in Italy, they claimed to have located a non-congruent political system where structure and culture do not match. Their emphasis on exclusion did not, however, extend to their discussion of women whose lower patterns of participation are deemed to be some way inevitable. However, because women's exclusion is never explicitly stated, it is never addressed.

*The Civic Culture* has been reviewed here to highlight how sexist assumptions influenced some early voting behaviour studies. The follow up volume, *The Civic Culture Revisited*, was published some years after the emergence of feminist political science. Interestingly, Almond and Verba's contributions clearly show a new dynamic in their approach to women (Almond and Verba 1980); they chose simply not mention them at all.

In the light of historic developments and Almond and Verba's rejection of the 'suffragettes' dream' (Almond and Verba. 1963: 334), one might expect to find a supplement to their analysis of sex in the 'revisited' volume. In Chapter one of the collection of critiques, Almond makes no reference to women or sex. In fact there are only two references to women, or sex, in the whole book. One reference to women is made by Carole Pateman in her philosophical critique of *The Civic Culture* (Pateman 1980).[6] In his chapter, Lijphart dismisses Pateman's position and defends Almond and Verba without even mentioning women (Lijphart 1980). The second reference to sex is a brief discussion about the changing perspective towards political participation amongst Catholic women in Germany. The whole of the women's movement seems to have gone entirely unnoticed!

To summarise, it can be clearly seen that *The Civic Culture* and its follow up, like the Michigan model, tended to conduct less than rigorous research when gender differences were evident.

## BUTLER AND STOKES AND *POLITICAL CHANGE IN BRITAIN*

David Butler and Donald Stokes extended the psychological/behavioural approach, developed by Campbell *et al.* to British voting behaviour (Butler and Stokes 1974). In the British context the partisan identification model was expanded to encompass occupational class. The model developed by Butler and Stokes became the foundational text of British voting behaviour. Their approach was fundamentally related to the Michigan model. In common with the Michigan model was the assumption that most people had little knowledge about politics and that their beliefs were formed in the main by socialisation processes. In the 1960s the assumption seemed valid because a great deal of parliamentary time was spent debating the technicalities of issues such as the effectiveness of nuclear deterrent and the consequences of the Cuban missile crisis. (Norris 1997) The complexities of these issues were considered, by Butler and Stokes, to be beyond the interest of the layman. (Butler and Stokes. 1974: 284) Butler and Stokes used data from the British Election Study (BES) to test their theories and found that voters failed to respond to the questions in a consistent way over the years in which they were surveyed. However, three-quarters of the respondents felt a strong affiliation to a political party, without any demonstrable link to the left–right scale. Therefore, parental class and party were believed to have a direct influence on voters' partisan identification. As in the Michigan model, party identification was understood to be a long-term factor explaining voting decisions. Actual vote choice in any given election could be affected by short-term factors, but these were underplayed. The model suggested that electoral change occurred as part of a gradual process of demographic change. Inhibited by the intergenerational nature of class influences, the lagged nature of economic structural changes and the immobility of labour, Butler and Stokes predicted that support for the Labour Party would increase in the 1970s and 1980s, as voters whose party identification was established prior to the emergence of the Labour Party died and left the electoral system. In the first edition of *Political Change in Britain*, Butler and Stokes suggested that the electorate might be becoming more volatile. In the second edition a whole chapter was devoted to this subject (Butler and Stokes 1974: Chapter nine).

The influence of the Michigan model and the British interpretation of it developed by Butler and Stokes have had a fundamental and lasting effect on later voting behaviour studies. The core issues raised and addressed in the literature focus on class and whether its primacy is defended or questioned. This is because class has undoubtedly had a profound influence on British politics. However, the emphasis on class is also a direct consequence of the influence of the partisan identification model. The partisan identification model predicted the relative stability of the British political system, particularly two-party politics, and the clear identification of the two associated voting blocs.

It is therefore not surprising that the emphasis in the voting behaviour literature is on critiques and defences of the approach advocated by Butler and Stokes. However, from a feminist perspective there is a problem. Class is understood to be the lead variable and hence even critics of Butler and Stokes tend to focus their analysis on class questions. The emphasis on class impedes a detailed theoretical account of the sex variable because this crosscuts all other demographic variables and its effects can be obscured at the aggregate level. A dual problem is that any analysis of women and sex found in the mainstream literature tends to be much less sophisticated and substantiated than the analysis of class factors. The historiography of voting behaviour studies shows how the early agenda-setting studies led to the sex variable becoming a side-issue. The sex variable was rarely considered in any detail until the discovery of the modern gender gap in the United States, when feminist studies of voting behaviour in Britain began to emerge.

The index of *Political Change in Britain* contains no direct references to sex, gender or women and none of the tables in the book contain the sex variable. The only occasion when Butler and Stokes consider the impact of possible sex differences is in their analysis of the early socialisation process. They state that 'when the direction of the mother's preference is distinguished from the father's it is plain that each parent, and not only the father, helps to form the nascent partisanship of the child' (Butler and Stokes. 1974: 32). They also indicate that the father's preference was more significant because it was more likely to be visible within the family; this claim was made without further justification or evidence. This is the only occasion when the effects of sex roles are analysed. It is notable that this interest in the role of women was based on the development of children.

## PARTISAN DEALIGNMENT

Critiques of Butler and Stokes' theories of social and partisan alignment can be described as belonging to the dealignment perspective. The dealignment perspective argues that the increase in third-party support evident in Britain, the reduction in the combined vote for the two main parties and the rise of nationalist support in Scotland and Wales all reflect a less cohesive and stable political system than was apparent in the 1950s and 1960s. Partisan and social dealignment are two distinct entities, although they are commonly linked in the literature. Norris explains that theories of social dealignment 'remain within the social psychological tradition, locating the explanation for the weakening two-party grip over the electorate in the changing character of the voting decision among individual electors' (Norris 1997: 85). Theories of partisan dealignment refer to the weakening of strong and stable party loyalties within the electorate.

In common with a great deal of British voting behaviour literature the dealignment school's predecessors were to be found in the United States. Norman Nie, Sidney Verba and John Petrocik found that party identification was a core feature of individual electoral choice but suggested that the bland politics of the Eisenhower era caused Campbell *et al.* to underestimate the influence of short-term factors (Nie, Verba and Petrocik 1979). They also found that, in the aftermath of controversies such as the Watergate scandal, party identification became a less crucial factor in vote choice and was less likely to be passed from generation to generation.

Bo Särlvik and Ivor Crewe's study of voting behaviour in the 1970s contains some references to sex and voting (Särlvik and Crewe 1983). Särlvik and Crewe present a page on sex, age and voting and found that 'the vote of men and women was virtually identical' (Särlvik and Crewe 1983: 91). Thus, the traditional gender gap, where women were more likely to vote for the Conservative Party than men, was not evident in the 1970s. Särlvik and Crewe did not look at the interaction between sex and age or sex and any other variables. Next they construct a tree diagram of the social determinates of Conservative vote in the 1979 election (Särlvik and Crewe 1983: 108). Sex and age are excluded from the tree because they only have a 'weak relationship to voting in the electorate as a whole and they emerge only in the form of slight variations in the sub-groups' (Särlvik and Crewe 1983: 110). Their analysis then focuses on the changing relationship between the working class and the Labour Party. Särlvik and Crewe moved beyond the tendency of the traditional literature and did not make unsubstantiated claims about women's behaviour and neither did they ignore the sex variable altogether. It would have been interesting to see what the 'slight variations in sub-groups' were since such effects can influence electoral outcomes. Overall, however, we see progress towards an approach that considers sex differences without using sexist assumptions.

Mark Franklin is frequently cited in British voting behaviour literature. He claims that, since 1964, the voting patterns in British general elections have changed significantly from the previously accepted norm (Franklin 1985). Franklin emphasises that Butler and Stokes' foundational work *Political Change in Britain*, was primarily concerned with class. He argues that changes in voting patterns in Britain have been attributed to class voting because it was the previously accepted lead variable. Franklin asserts that class has never been investigated by a standard measure. He asserts that, in combination with economic growth, government policies have changed the demographic make-up of British society, for example, changes in tenancy law, property ownership, educational reform and policies to encourage the extension of trade-union membership to white collar workers. Franklin indicates that changes in class structure account for approximately half the shift in party support. He attributes changes in electoral behaviour to the fact that Labour became 'less appealing to groups traditionally supported by it' (Franklin 1985: 176). This, according to Franklin, explains the reduction in the class basis of voting and the increased volatility and self-expressive nature of the electorate.

From a feminist perspective it is interesting to note that there are no references to sex, gender or women or men in the index of Franklin's book. When Franklin discusses the effect of parental party and parental class he makes no reference to women or men and there is no suggestion that family members may have different backgrounds. This omission is important because his analysis uses head-of-household statistics. Franklin's work is based on an analysis of the influence of class, even though he questions its salience. He indicates that class was the 'previously accepted predominant variable' a statement that seemed to imply that such emphasis may have been erroneous. However, it does not encourage him to include new variables to analyse voting behaviour. In Franklin's work, women are totally subsumed under the family label because their husbands determine their class.

Richard Rose and Ian McAllister's perspective has much in common with Franklin, Särlvik and Crewe (Rose and McAllister 1986). They also address the approach begun by Butler and Stokes. They claim that 'the old class equals party model is no more, if it ever was' (Rose and McAllister 1986: 45). The basis of their argument is that the previously assumed ignorance of the electorate has been supplanted by a rational reasoning behind voting, as a process of partisan dealignment has taken place. Partisan dealignment, the decline of strong individual association with one party, has a corollary, social dealignment, associated with a weakening of class structures. The combination of these two elements is theorised to account for the de-stabilising of the two-party system, which was a fundamental feature of the traditional British model. Rose and McAllister pay significantly more attention to gender than many of their predecessors. They address one of the fundamental, gender-related, problems with the traditional approach to class. This problem results from the use of head-of-household statistics. They use the innovation recommended by Anthony Heath, Roger Jowell and John Curtice in *How Britain Votes* (Heath, Jowell and Curtice 1985). This classification is dependent on classifying the occupations of each individual rather than under the occupation of the head of household. However, they appear, also, to take a backward step with regard to the sex variable. They state that 'it can be argued that occupational class should be assigned to each person individually, however, this neo-liberal emphasis upon the autonomy of the individual ignores the significance of the family as a social and economic unit' (Rose and McAllister 1986: 45). Rose and McAllister then drop the gendered statistics and reinstate the head-of-household statistic. They justify the decision by claiming that no sex effects were evident in the data. They explain the lack of a sex effect with the statement 'very few women in the electorate today came of age without the right to vote, therefore gender differences arising from past history are likely to be negligible' (Rose and McAllister 1986: 169).

Rose and McAllister consider sex and vote but state that any association could be spurious because women tend to live longer than men and older people tend to

A. Table 4.6: Gender and voting

| Matrix of determination | Conservative | Alliance | Labour |
|---|---|---|---|
| Housewives | 9 | 4 | 5 |
| Working women | 15 | 10 | 10 |
| Men | 21 | 11 | 14 |

B. Table 4.6 with totals[7]

| Matrix of determination | Conservative | Alliance | Labour | Total |
|---|---|---|---|---|
| Housewives | 9 (50%) | 4 (22.2%) | 5 (27.8%) | 18 (100%) |
| Working women | 15 (42.9%) | 10 (28.55%) | 10 (28.55%) | 35 (100%) |
| Men | 21 (45.7%) | 11 (23.9%) | 14 (30.4%) | 46 (100%) |
| Total | 45 | 25 | 29 | 99 |

C. Percentage voting for the three main political parties, by sex[8]

| Sex | Conservative | Alliance | Labour |
|---|---|---|---|
| Female | 24% | 14% | 15% |
| Male | 21% | 11% | 14% |

be more conservative (Rose and McAllister 1986: 70). Their observation appears to be a strong argument for studying sex effects within sub-sectors, such as generational cohorts (analysis that has been undertaken by Pippa Norris).

When discussing aggregate-level data Rose and McAllister conclude that 'women divide their votes in virtually the same way as men' (Rose and McAllister 1986: 70). The tables created by Rose and McAllister present a sophisticated breakdown of the data. Overall the percentage point differences between the way men and women vote are not enormous but are interesting.

The tables above illustrate how aggregate level similarities can obscure sub-sector differences and how the failure to present statistics properly can prohibit accurate analysis. Rose and McAllister's table (A) does not permit comparison. The table (B) with the total additions is clearer. In this table it is apparent that housewives are the most Conservative by a margin of 8 per cent above working women. It is also interesting to note that men were slightly more Conservative as a whole than working women. The overall support for the Labour Party was relatively consistent, undermining the idea that working women would be more inclined to vote Labour than housewives because of their contact with trade unions. In fact, the most striking pattern is that 6 per cent more working women voted for the Liberal Democrat Alliance than housewives did and 5 per cent more working women voted for the Alliance than men did. The percentage differences are not high enough to suggest that sex has a radical effect on voting behaviour when housewives and working women are controlled for, but the percentages are certainly large enough to warrant further investigation into the impact of the sex variable. Yet Rose and McAllister conclude that 'when voting patterns of men, working women and housewives are compared, controlling for head of household's class, there is virtually no effect of gender or employment' (Rose and McAllister 1986: 71). Rose and McAllister must be commended for studying gender effects below the aggregate level. However, their dismissal of its significance may be doubtful. Although the percentage differences are small it is possible that similar differences occur throughout other sub-sectors, such as religion, race, age, education, nature of employment. These differences might combine to provide a complex but significant gender effect.

## DEALIGNMENT?

*How Britain Votes* is a critique of theories of dealignment and issue-voting models (Heath, Jowell and Curtice 1985). In their study of the 1983 general election Heath *et al.* claim that there was no evidence of class dealignment. They also assert that class dealignment effects were found by other researchers because of misinterpretation of short-term trends. They develop what they term the 'interactionist' model. This approach is not strictly bottom up but includes government interaction with voter perceptions of class. In common with its predecessor, the Michigan model, this interactionist model is sceptical about the capacity of voters to make rational choices regarding complex political issues. Their model fuelled a heated debate within the electoral studies literature, which included a proliferation of articles bouncing from one school to the other (Crewe 1986; Heath, Jowell and Curtice 1987).

Heath *et al.* state that women are often subsumed under the head of household's class; they suggest that married women's own workplace experience should be identified (Heath *et al.* 1987: 22). They present data which illustrates the over-representation of women in routine non-manual work and their under-representation in the salariat and blue-collar work. They conclude, however, that this reallocation has virtually no effect on their conclusions regarding class differences. Despite this, they do note that working-class women were more likely to vote for the Alliance than working-class men were. This is in keeping with the evidence found by Rose and McAllister.

Heath *et al.* find an interesting gender gap within the working class which becomes more pronounced when technical workers are analysed, where women were marginally less likely to vote Labour and more likely to vote for the Alliance (Heath *et al.* 1987: 23). Overall Heath *et al.*'s analysis is thoughtful about the possible impact of sex or gender on vote and they are careful to consider potential sub-group differences. However, they don't consider the effects of education or age. They fail to do this because class is found to be the lead variable at an aggregate level for many of the dependent variables they are interested in. The assumption is therefore made that class will continue to be the most significant factor within sub-sectors. It may be the case that this hypothesis is true, but Heath *et al.* undertake insufficient analysis to support this contention, with regard to gender.

Following *How Britain Votes* Heath *et al.* published *The British Voter:*

*1964–1987*, which is centrally concerned with exploring social and political sources of electoral change in Britain (Heath *et al.* 1991). The key question is whether the electorate has become more volatile. Heath *et al.* sought to investigate first whether new ideological cleavages had emerged, which had become more significant than the previously dominant cleavages based on social class. Secondly, they asked whether the Conservative Party had successfully shaped social structures in its favour and then cite the data on the decline in two-party support, from 97 per cent of votes cast in 1951 to 78 per cent in 1987. They then research possible reasons for the decline in electoral support for the Labour Party, e.g. the 15 per cent reduction in the manual labour force between 1951 and 1981; the increase in owner-occupancy from 31 to 63 per cent between 1951 and 1986 and the increase in the number of school leavers with academic qualifications.

Heath *et al.* claim that *How Britain Votes* demonstrates that Labour's losses in 1983 were generally not class specific. Instead they suggest that the result reflected trendless fluctuation rather than dealignment. They further argue that a contention that social class is less important requires the identification of alternative social cleavages based on 'sectoral location' (Heath *et al.* 1991: 5). They contend that the dealignment perspective suggests a relatively passive role for political parties. They are interested in the possibility that parties may be able to influence structural change. For example, the possible psychological effects on working-class members of the electorate of the sale of council houses. They cite Norris's suggestion that Thatcherite anti-inflationary policies led to increased unemployment and may have increased political apathy amongst traditional Labour supporters, through the absence of shopfloor activity. The analysis of electoral volatility concludes that 'different measures tell different stories' (Heath *et al.* 1991: 19). They assert that there was a decline in party identification from 1964 but that there has also been an increase in the stickiness between Labour voting and non-voting. On the 'rational electorate' Heath *et al.* surmise that voters were equally rational in the 1960s and were influenced rather than constrained by childhood socialisation (Heath *et al.* 1991: 44). They emphasise the importance of understanding the 'multi-dimensional character of social and political values when assessing theories previously outlined' (Heath *et al.* 1991: 173). They explain that attitudes toward privatisation and the free market fit on the traditional left-right scale, whilst issues like capital punishment exist outside of it. Their research into issue preference is then conducted around the framework of the left-right scale and the liberal/authoritarian scale controlling for a number of demographic variables. Analysis of the data leads them to conclude that class was the most dominant variable on the left-right scale, whilst education was the most dominant on the liberal/authoritarian scale.

Heath *et al.* show that the young are significantly more left-wing than the old and that women are more left-wing than men. This is the first time a table in this text has included the sex variable; there is no explanation for its previous exclusion, or its sudden appearance.

This table is included in a discussion in the notes about the relationship between religion and attitudes. It is included because religion was found to be a

Table 11.2: Regression analysis of attitudes towards left-right and liberal/authoritarian issues[9]

| Independent variables | Dependent variables | |
| --- | --- | --- |
| | Left-Right scale | Lib/Auth scale |
| Class | 0.2** | -0.04 |
| Father's class | 0.13** | -0.03 |
| Housing tenure | 0.13** | -0.02 |
| Trade union membership | 0.07** | 0.02 |
| Region | 0.10** | 0.00 |
| Education | 0.01 | -0.28** |
| Churches of England and Scotland | 0.04* | 0.01 |
| Other Churches | -0.05* | -0.08** |
| Age | 0.14 | 0.03 |
| Sex | 0.06** | 0.04 |

* Significant at the 0.05 per cent level.   ** Significant at the 0.01 per cent level.

Table 11.9n: Regression analysis of attitudes towards abortion

| Independent variables | Standardised regression coefficients |
| --- | --- |
| Class | 0.01 |
| Father's class | -0.03 |
| Housing tenure | -0.04 |
| Trade union membership | 0.02 |
| Region | -0.07** |
| Education | -0.04 |
| Churches of England and Scotland | 0.04 |
| Other Churches | 0.17** |
| Age | 0.11 |
| Sex | 0.08** |

* Significant at the 5 per cent level.
** Significant at the 1 per cent level.
(Table 11.9n, located in the notes also includes the sex variable (*ibid*. pp. 183))

significant variable with regards to abortion. Sex, however, is also significant and has a larger than average standardised regression coefficient, this point is not raised or discussed by Heath *et al*.

Heath *et al*. conclude from the table that the 'people who are opposed to nuclear weapons and nuclear power tend to be young, female and irreligious' (Heath *et al*. 1991: 189). No further reference is made to sex, and no possible explanations are provided for the sex differences found. They then return to class issues, stating that the social characteristics of anti-nuclear voters are relatively similar to those of traditional left-wingers. The survey of Heath *et al*.'s research shows that by 1991 the analysis of sex differences had moved to the mainstream but only as a control variable rather than as an object of discussion.

Table 12.2: Regression analysis of attitudes toward nuclear and countryside issues (*ibid*. pp. 189)

| Independent variables | Dependent variables | |
|---|---|---|
| | Nuclear scale | Countryside scale |
| Class | 0.04 | -0.06* |
| Father's class | 0.07** | 0.01 |
| Housing tenure | 0.05* | -0.08** |
| Trade union membership | 0.06** | 0.01 |
| Region | 0.04* | 0.14** |
| Education | -0.06** | 0.12** |
| Churches of England and Scotland | -0.08** | 0.02 |
| Other Churches | 0.05** | -0.04* |
| Age | 0.09** | 0.04* |
| Sex | 0.14** | -0.04* |
| $R^2$ | 0.06 | 0.07 |
| N | 2666 | 2623 |

* Significant at the 5 per cent level.
** Significant at the 1 per cent level.

In their final chapter Heath *et al*. assert that they 'doubt if the social psychology of the electorate has changed much if at all over the last twenty five years' (Heath *et al*. 1991: 200). They do note some important changes including the increase of the middle classes, the decrease in participation in organised religion, the increase in levels of education and an increase in equality. They also note that the party system has expanded to include a third party. There is no explicit mention of the second wave of feminism and the increased numbers of women participating in the paid work force. Much of their data demonstrates significant gender differences but this is largely ignored. This book fails to provide any account of gender and voting, even though the research indicates its relevance.

## THE RADICAL MODEL

Dunleavy and Husbands' *British Democracy at the Crossroads* is written from a perspective which is

> sceptical of the tradition inaugurated by Butler and Stokes and continued by other writers, in which large research monographs on citizen attitudes are produced with only a minimum specification of the events that gave rise to them (Dunleavy and Husbands 1985: IVXII).

Dunleavy and Husbands name their approach 'the radical model' and place it in direct opposition to the party-identification model and the issue-voting model. They reject individual-level analysis in favour of aggregate social phenomena.

They state that they do not expect to find any 'one for one correspondence between social-structural influences on alignments and voter attitudes' (Dunleavey and Husbands 1985: 19). They claim that there are a wide variety of influences including class, economic activity, sectoral location and gender. Their explanation for dealignment is structural, described as a by-product of changes in the social basis of political life. They suggest that as people's interests become more complex they lose the shelter provided by a coherent interest and become aware of dominant ideological messages. They assert that their model revolves around political feasibility, the scope of which is largely defined by the leadership of political parties. Time lags between shifts in social movements and political representation of them are explained by the constraints made upon the leadership by the ideological beliefs of party members.

Dunleavy and Husbands criticise Butler and Stokes for assigning all married women their husband's occupational class even if they were working. They also state that 'most comparisons of men's and women's voting patterns do not even control for occupational class. More contentious researchers proceed on the basis that, since the primacy of occupational class has been established, we simply compare male and female voting within the same class' (Dunleavy and Husbands 1985: 124).

Dunleavy and Husbands identify aggregate differences that are much smaller than those within occupational classes. They then cite some problems concerned with comparing voting choice within occupational class. Women are less successful at attaining career advancement than men due to sexism and sexist practices and particularly if they get married and stop work for a period to care for children. Therefore, they contend that gender positions are logically prior to occupational class. Accordingly, they assess the impact of social class in place of occupational class.

From their data, Dunleavy and Husbands conclude that, among women, it is the manual/non-manual distinction that is critical. They also say that 'our results suggest a need for further investigation'(Dunleavy and Husbands 1985: 128).This

Table 6.4: Voting in the 1983 general election by gender and Registrar-General's occupational class (in percentages)

| Occupational class | Gender | Labour | Conservative | Alliance | C/B[10] | N |
|---|---|---|---|---|---|---|
| Professional etc. | Men | 9 | 65 | 26 | +56 | 85 |
| | Women | 8 | 57 | 36 | +49 | 76 |
| Intermediate and junior non-manual | Men | 26 | 40 | 34 | +14 | 70 |
| | Women | 19 | 55 | 26 | +36 | 115 |
| Skilled manual | Men | 39 | 32 | 29 | -7 | 134 |
| | Women | 33 | 43 | 24 | +10 | 138 |
| Less skilled manual | Men | 42 | 29 | 30 | -13 | 77 |
| | Women | 53 | 28 | 19 | -25 | 92 |
| All classes | Men | 30 | 40 | 30 | +10 | 366 |
| | Women | 29 | 45 | 25 | +16 | 421 |

Table 6.5: Voting in the 1983 general election by gender and social class

| Social class | Gender | Labour | Conservative | Alliance | C/B | N |
|---|---|---|---|---|---|---|
| Manual | Men | Women | 52 | 27 | 20 | -25 |
| | Women | Men | 41 | 29 | 30 | -12 |
| Non-manual | Men | Women | 15 | 53 | 32 | +38 |
| | Women | Men | 26 | 36 | 38 | +10 |
| Controllers of labour | Men | Women | 16 | 61 | 24 | +45 |
| | Women | Men | 15 | 56 | 29 | +41 |
| Employers | Men | Women | 20 | 64 | 16 | +44 |
| | Women | Men | 10 | 71 | 19 | +61 |
| All classes | Men | Women | 29 | 46 | 25 | +17 |
| | Women | Men | 30 | 41 | 30 | +11 |

is an interesting and detailed examination of gender differences in one sub-sector, but, as Dunleavy and Husbands state, the primacy of class is 'known' and other sub-sectors are bypassed. However, the primacy of class at aggregate levels does not guarantee that it will be the lead variable within sub-sectors. A thorough examination would require an analysis as outlined above but would be extended to include religious, regional, racial, educational and other sub-sectors. It would also necessarily include a theoretically based hypothesis to explain and describe any gender differences.


## SUMMARY

The story of sex and the study of voting behaviour illustrated in this chapter is a gradual transition, from overtly sexist practice to benign neglect to the current state of the discipline, where gender is usually more thoughtfully theorised. The critique also highlights that effective analysis of sex differences requires the use of theories of gender difference to generate testable hypotheses.

This book hopes to contribute to the literature by attempting to establish whether feminist theory can add anything to our understanding of voting behaviour in Britain. The cross-cutting nature of the sex variable means that complex theories of gender must be employed to understand how and why men and women's lives are different and how this difference impacts upon political preferences and, ultimately, vote choice.

## NOTES

1   This is an oversimplified version of Almond and Verba's theory but is sufficient for the explanatory purposes required here.
2   The information in this table is identical to that provided by Almond and Verba in all but the column marked gender gap. This figure is my own addition and was not presented in the original table.
3   The gender gap figures are my addition to the table and are calculated by subtracting the male percentages from the female, in the case of PPDi the primary education figure is subtracted from the secondary education figure. This is helpful when attempting to assess the influence of education on the gender gap.
4   GG is an abbreviation for the term gender gap and PPD is an abbreviation for the term percentage point difference.
5   Percentage difference in gender gap percentages between those with a primary education, or less and those with a secondary education or more, by country. This statistic is designed to show whether it can be claimed that this data suggests a relationship between the level of education and the likelihood of discussing politics in relation to sex. It is calculated by subtracting the primary education figure from the secondary education figure for each of the countries surveyed. This statistic is an addition to the original data and was not presented by Almond and Verba.
6   In her philosophical critique, Carole Pateman questions the theoretical foundations of *The Civic Culture*. She affirms that Almond and Verba's treatment of liberal democracy as a system and their attempt to establish a relationship between it and political culture was an admirable goal. However, she argues that they failed because they overlooked classic participatory liberal theory and were prepared to accept low levels of participation in some groups. She asserts that 'the most striking finding in *The Civic Culture* is that the civic culture is systematically divided along lines of class and sex' (Pateman 1980: 60). Pateman contends that Almond and Verba develop circular arguments that fail to provide insight into causation. In Chapter 2, Lijphart dismisses Pateman's contention by saying that both culture and system are first observed and only then related. Lijphart's is an insufficient retort, because assumptions about what it means to live in a liberal democracy are made throughout the empirical investigation of culture. For example, the open family is a notion developed to explain greater female activity in the US and the UK, based on the assumption that the public and private realms are separate; this assumption is not developed inductively. Liberal democracy is the very basis by which culture is evaluated.
7   The addition of totals was not present in Rose and McAllister's text.
8   This is not how the table is presented by Rose and McAllister.
9   This table contains exactly the same data as Table 11.2 in *The British Voter* p. 175.
10  C/B stands for Conservative lead over Labour.

# chapter three | gender ideology and issue preference[1]

This chapter is designed to determine whether there is any evidence to suggest that men and women might have different attitudes to politics. Should there be differences in men and women's political priorities or between the priorities of subgroups of men and women then we find some confirmation that a 'women's interest' exists, if perhaps in nascent or unarticulated form. This chapter conceives of women's interests as context- and group-specific and not essentialist in nature.

## DO MEN AND WOMEN ORGANISE THEIR POLITICAL VIEWS IN THE SAME WAY?

This chapter is concerned with the ways that men's and women's political views could differ. Men and women may hold different views about political issues. For example, men may be more likely to support military intervention than women. Alternatively, men and women may have differing political priorities. There may be no observable difference in the position men and women take on issues but they may view them as being more or less important. For example, women may prioritise spending on education, whilst men might be more likely to prioritise tax cuts (Box-Steffensmeir, DeBoef and Lin 1997; Chaney, Alvarez and Nagler 1998; Kornhauser 1987; Kornhauser 1997). Testing for these two possible locations of difference, or similarity, requires different methods of analysis. Issue location is relatively easy to assess with readily available national datasets. A simple test would be to compare the mean responses of the sexes to issue-related questions. Issue preference is more difficult to measure. Ideally, issue preference should be accessed by direct questions asking respondents to rank issues in an order of priority. The British Election Study (BES) has asked respondents to do this a number of times since its inception. An alternative approach is to use statistical tests to measure the impact of specific issues on vote choice. This chapter does not attempt to provide a comprehensive model of voting by sex but uses vote choice as a means to identify issue preference. There have been comprehensive studies that compare the attitude positions of the sexes over a vast range of issues. This chapter focuses specifically on measures of ideology and issues that have been theorised to be of special significance to women (Shapiro and Mahajan 1986).

The discussion will proceed by examining issue preference by looking at responses to an ordered question in the 2001 BES by sex and sex/age. The analysis then moves to issue location; mean differences between the sexes are compared for different measures of political ideology. Ideology is conceived as an underlying mechanism through which attitudes are framed. Ideology is commonly measured by a respondent's left–right position. Finally issue preference is re-examined by assessing which measures have the most impact on the vote choice of respondents by sex and generation. There is variation in the questions asked throughout the British Election Study series and, due to availability of suitable questions, the last two stages of the analysis are conducted on the 1997 BES and not the 2001 BES.

## GENDER DIFFERENCES IN IDEOLOGY: POINTERS FROM THE GENDER GAP LITERATURE

Having identified the two possible locations of gender difference in ideology it is necessary to consider two more important questions. Why should we be interested in gender differences in ideology and what reasons are there for theorising that they might exist? The answers to these questions stem from two sources; feminist theory and feminist empirical research. A brief précis of the two approaches is presented below.

From a theoretical perspective, as outlined in Chapter one, analysis of gender and political attitudes can be used to test whether there is evidence to support one pillar of Anne Phillips' arguments for fairer representation of women in parliament (Phillips 1994; Phillips 1995). Phillips argues that women may have interests that remain unarticulated in a male-dominated political system and that more women representatives are necessary if that interest is to be defined, voiced and acted upon.

For Phillips' argument to be sustained, I contend that there should, at the very least, be some evidence to suggest heterogeneity between the political priorities of the sexes. Differences between the sexes within sub-sectors of the population would be sufficient to support the Phillips case. They might be theorised to exist because of the cross-cutting nature of the sex variable, which interacts with all other demographic factors. Thus we might not expect the interests of middle-class and working-class women, for example, to be identical, but we might expect them to be different from middle-class and working-class men, respectively.

Whilst this study seeks to address a specific feature of theoretical arguments about the representation of women, it also attempts to test feminist empirical research, namely Pippa Norris's discovery of a gender generation gap in political attitudes and behaviour (Norris 1999). As described in Chapter one, Norris has demonstrated that the traditional gender gap, where women were more likely than men to vote for the Conservative Party in Britain, has reversed in generations born since the Second World War. Thus, in generations born prior to the Second World War the traditional gap holds, but women born after the Second World War are more likely to vote for the Labour Party than men of the same generations. Norris and Inglehart suggest that the gender generation gap is an international phenomenon and is part of a global developmental pattern where women are becoming more left-leaning than men (Inglehart and Norris 1999). This chapter will test whether Norris and Inglehart's gender generation gap is evident in political attitudes in Britain.

As described in Chapter one, in the United States the modern gender gap in vote choice has been apparent at the aggregate level, with more women than men voting for democratic candidates in presidential elections since 1980 (Norris 2001). This development has generated some detailed and insightful research into gender and voting patterns. In some cases feminist theories such as Carol Gilligan's 'ethics of care' (Gilligan 1982) have been operationalised to test whether women are more altruistic than men in their motivations for vote choice. From this perspective women are theorised to favour increased taxation and spending on welfare provision, whilst men are theorised to be more likely to be governed by pocket-book voting or income tax levels. The alternative model of gender difference applied in the United States is akin to feminist standpoint theory or, alternatively, rational choice theory. Women are thought to be more inclined to support increased spending on welfare than men because women are more likely to be the beneficiaries of such provision or because of their specific experiences as women (Bendyna and Lake 1994; Box-Steffensmeir, DeBoef and Lin 1997; Chaney, Alvarez and Nagler 1998; Mueller 1988).

Whether the rational choice or 'ethics of care' approach is preferred, the hypothesis generated is that women will be more likely than men to support political parties that offer increased spending on welfare. If the gender generation gap evident in Britain can be explained by either theory, we would expect attitudes towards welfare provision, particularly health and education, to impact upon the voting choices of younger women. This hypothesis will be tested in the third and final sections of analysis.

However, the model is further complicated by the theoretical explanations for the traditional gender gap in voting, where women, in the past, were more likely to vote for right-leaning political parties than men. In the United States there is a tendency for religious Southern women to be more inclined to vote for the Republican Party than other women. It is possible that the traditional gender gap in voting might be better explained by reference to traditional values or moral conservatism.

Norris and Inglehart attribute global patterns of change in the gender gap to 'long-term structural and cultural trends, that have transformed women's lives and have gradually produced a realignment in women's politics in post-industrial societies' (Inglehart and Norris 2000). Women's location in the home and the influence of religiousness and the church are considered to be likely explanations for the traditional gender gap, hence the emphasis on moral conservatism as a predictor of vote choice. In order to include a measure of moral conservatism in the analysis Heath *et al.*'s liberal–authoritarian scale is utilised and its impact on the vote choice of the sexes compared (Heath, Evans and Martin 1993).

## EVIDENCE OF DISTINCTIVE WOMEN'S INTERESTS?

From a brief reminder of the gender gap literature we can see how left–right ideology and issue preference are theorised to play a crucial role in explaining the vote choices of men and women internationally. This emphasis on ideology warrants an examination of whether the theorised differences in attitude between the sexes are apparent in responses to the BES.[2]

In her study of the Swedish Riksdag, Wängnerud addresses the very element of Phillips's argument for quota systems that is relevant to this study. Wängnerud utilises an ordered question to test Phillips's claims (Wängnerud 2000). The question is 'thinking about this year's election, is there any issue or issues that is especially important to you when it comes to choosing which party you are going to vote for?'. Wängnerud is able to compare men's and women's responses to this question over time, from 1982 to 1994. She found that 'jobs and the environment were two of the policy areas most frequently mentioned by both the sexes in the period studied... Family policy is an important area among female voters, but not among male voters... Social policy and health care is given higher priority by female voters than by male voters... The economy and taxes are prioritised more highly by male voters than by female voters' (Wängnerud 2000). These findings are similar to those that have been emanating from the United States. From this data analysis Wängnerud concludes that 'the analysis underpins the view that there are grounds for adopting a gender perspective on the political process. We obtain confirmation that the theory of the politics of presence involves pivotal issues in representative democracy' (Wängnerud 2000).

A question asking the respondent to order preferences is available in the 2001 British Election Study. The question asks respondents to specify their most important election issue.[3] In the Swedish voter survey respondents were asked to specify three issues, which led to more illuminating results. The responses to the 2001 BES question, by sex, are outlined in Table 3.1. A chi-square test was conducted and was significant at the 0.001 level. The test shows that there is a less than 1 in 1000 chance that the variables sex and most important election issue are independent of each other. In later analysis the individual issues are considered separately.

In all of the categories there is some difference between the sexes, the most striking involve educational standards, the state of the economy and the National Health Service. Nearly twice as many women as men prioritise education, with 7.5 per cent of men naming education as their top priority compared with 14 per cent of women. Women were 5 per cent more likely than men to state the NHS as their top priority; 26 per cent of men named the NHS as their top priority compared with 31 per cent of women. Men were more likely to state that the economy was

Table 3.1: Respondents' most important election issue, by sex, 2001

| Issue | Male | Female |
|---|---|---|
| Britain's membership in the European Monetary Union | 9.5% | 6.6% |
| Britain's relations with the European Union | 5.0% | 2.7% |
| Law and order | 3.6% | 2.9% |
| **Educational standards** | **7.5%** | **14.2%** |
| Environment | 0.5% | 1.0% |
| **National Health Service** | **25.6%** | **31.3%** |
| Inflation, prices generally | 0.5% | 0.3% |
| Public transport | 0.5% | 0.7% |
| Taxation | 5.3% | 3.1% |
| **State of the economy** | **4.7%** | **0.8%** |
| Unemployment | 0.9% | 0.7% |
| Respondent's standard of living | 1.6% | 1.2% |
| Price of petrol | 1.2% | 0.5% |
| Foot and mouth disease | 0.3% | 1.2% |
| Immigration/asylum seekers | 2.2% | 1.7% |
| Pensions | 2.4% | 3.5% |
| Other | 13.0% | 9.2% |
| None | 5.6% | 5.1% |
| Don't know | 10.2% | 13.2% |
| Total | 100% n=1455 | 100% n=1560 |

the most important election issue than women by 4 per cent, with 5 per cent of men prioritising the economy compared to 1 per cent of women. When the respondents who prioritised education and the NHS were combined, 46 per cent of women prioritised one of these issues compared with 34 per cent of men. The interpretation of these results is considerably illuminated when they are broken down by sex and age. The relationship between issue priority, age and sex is presented in the form of bar charts in Figures 3.1 to 3.6 below.

An obvious interpretation of Figures 3.1 and 3.2 is that women are more likely to prioritise education when they are of child-bearing age and that they are more likely to emphasise the NHS as they approach pensionable age.[4] However further exploration of these two theories is not possible because the 2001 British Election Study does not contain information on parenthood. These results have some implications for the gender generation gap theory. We have seen that prioritising spending on health and education is linked to votes for Democratic candidates in the US case. In Britain, however, older women are theorised to be more likely to vote for the Conservative Party than men or young women. If the theory is applicable to both countries we would expect the older women who prioritise the NHS to vote for the Labour Party. In relation to ideological position, it might be that the

Figure 3.1: Respondents who named educational standards as the most important election issue, by age and sex, 2001BES

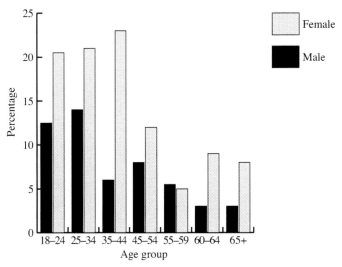

The difference between the sexes is significant at the 0.05 level for the respondents aged between 24 and 34, at the 0.01 level for the over 65s and at the 0.001 level for the respondents aged between 35 and 44 (chi-square test).

Figure 3.2: Respondents who named the NHS as the most important election issue, by age and sex, 2001BES

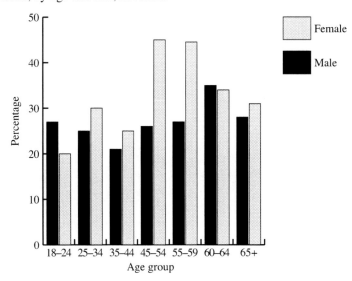

The difference between the sexes is significant at the 0.01 level for the respondents aged 55 to 59 and at the 0.001 level for the respondents aged between 45 and 54 (chi-square test).

Figure 3.3: Respondents who chose Britain's relations with the European Union or European Monetary Union as their most important election issue, by age group and sex, from the 2001 BES

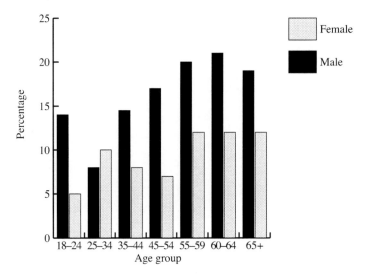

The difference between the sexes is significant at the 0.05 level for respondents aged 18 to 24, 35 to 44, 55 to 59 and in the over 65s. The difference is significant at the 0.01 level for respondents aged between 45 and 54 (chi-square test).

liberal–authoritarian scale is better able to explain the votes of older women than the left–right scale. Alternatively, there may be external factors inhibiting the Labour vote amongst older women, such as a perception that it is a masculine institution. Alternatively they may believe that the Conservative Party will provide the best healthcare policies.

Figure 3.3 demonstrates that, on average, European issues are more important to the vote choices of men than women.

Taxation was most important to men aged twenty-five to thirty-four. This finding supports the gender gap thesis, which suggests that women will be most interested in welfare provision, whilst men might be more likely to be governed by pocket-book politics. The economy was more important to men than women in every age group, except the under-twenty-fives, a finding that also supports theories about gender difference from feminist theory and research in the United States.

Figure 3.6 indicates that immigration or asylum was most important to men aged eighteen to twenty-four, something that was not predicted by feminist theory or research. Some of the percentage differences represented in Figures 3.1–3.6 are relatively small; others are larger; many of the gaps are statistically significant.

There is evidence to suggest that sex interacts with age or generation to produce effects on attitude. In order to establish whether these are age or generation

Figure 3.4: Respondents who stated that taxation was their most important election issue, by age group and sex, from the 2001 BES

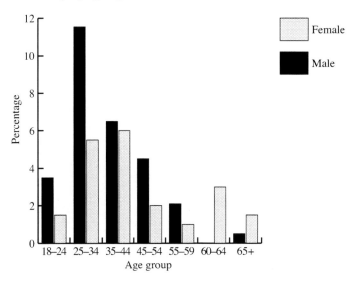

The difference between the sexes is significant at the 0.01 level for respondents aged between 25 and 34 (chi-square test).

Figure 3.5: Respondents who stated that the economy was their most important election issue, by age group and sex, from the 2001 BES

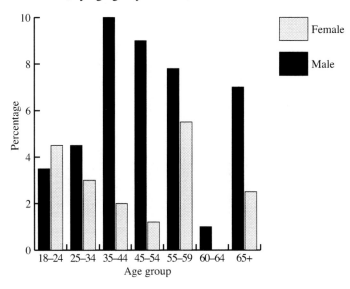

The difference between the sexes is significant at the 0.001 level for respondents aged between 35 and 54 and at the 0.05 level for respondents aged over 65 (chi-square test).

Figure 3.6: Respondents who stated that immigration or asylum was their most important election issue, by age and sex, from the 2001 BES

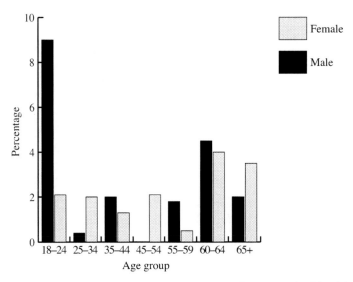

The difference between the sexes is statistically significant at the 0.05 level for the respondents aged 18–24.

effects it would be necessary to conduct a time-series or long-term panel analysis, which is not possible using the British Election Study because there are too few ordered questions. These initial results do not refute the gender generation gap thesis and the differences are large enough to suggest that more rigorous research is needed in order to determine true differences and discount random error.

These findings contribute to the research of Phillips and Wängnerud outlined in the introduction to this chapter. If Wängnerud's claims are accepted, then the gender dimensions of the issue priority scale illustrated in Table 3.1 and Figures 3.1–3.6 are sufficient to support one element of Anne Phillips' argument for sex quotas in Britain.

## GENDER AND IDEOLOGY

This section is designed to assess first whether men and women or men and women from different sub-sectors hold the same ideological positions and, second, to test whether the measures of ideological position commonly employed in studies of voting behaviour in Britain are equally applicable to both sexes. Previous research has highlighted the potentially gendered nature of attitude positions.

A single, broadly defined liberal-conservative ideological continuum almost certainly cannot be applied…to women, if it ever could. (*cf.* Nie *et al.* 1979;

Miller and Levitan 1976; Converse 1964). It is possible that men and women – or different generations of them – organize their attitudes and opinions in different ways. Compassion, traditional values, regulation and protection and force and violence may be the major dimensions that help structure women's attitudes, others may apply to men (Shapiro and Mahajan 1986: 45).

Shapiro and Mahajan neatly encapsulate the issues that need to be addressed within a study of gender and ideology (Shapiro and Mahajan 1986). The core question 'whether men and women systematically organize their political views and choices in the same way,' is easily transferable to a British context and the debate about whether electors structure their opinions at all is an international one.

Many studies of the gender gap in voting in the United States found that women will prioritise healthcare and education spending and that such an emphasis can explain why they are more likely than men to vote for the Democratic candidates in presidential elections (Box-Steffensmeir, DeBoef and Lin 1997; Chaney, Alvarez and Nagler 1998; Kornhauser 1987; Kornhauser 1997). Implicit in the argument is the assumption that the indicators of the traditional left–right scale might not adequately explain the left-leaning tendencies of women. Thus, we might predict that the traditional left–right scale should not have as large an impact on women's voting as men's. Instead, indicators that specifically address health and education should have greater explanatory power in regard to the voting choice of women. The prediction outlined above is refined by the introduction of the liberal–authoritarian scale. The research from the United States, which indicates that women should prioritise healthcare and education, contains a parallel dimension. Where Southern religious women are more likely to identify with the Republican Party, their motivations are thought to be based in moral conservatism rather than left–right position. This brings us to a second hypothesis, that older and/or religious women's voting behaviour will be better explained by the liberal–authoritarian scale than by the left–right scale. Testing the liberal–authoritarian hypothesis will be relatively straightforward. As well as applying the standard scales and testing for differences between the sexes we must ensure that the scales are not themselves gendered. Each item within the scale must be considered and

Table 3.2: Mean difference in self-placement on the Left-Right scale

| Year | Birth cohort | Gender gap |
|------|--------------|------------|
| 1983 BES | 1907–1946 | -0.06 |
| | 1947–1966 | +0.09 |
| | Total | -0.03 |
| 2001 BES | 1907–1946 | -0.18 |
| | 1947–1986 | +0.21* |
| | Total | +0.01 |

*Significant at the 0.05 level (one-tailed ANOVA)

we must theorise whether there might be gender implications. So the first step in the analysis is to assess whether the scales are gendered and the second step is to see whether their effect on voting behaviour is different for men and women.

The hypothesised ideological differences between the sexes have been out-lined above. In the following section different measures of ideology are tested for sex and gender relationships.

One method of measuring ideological position is to look at respondents' self-placement on the left–right scale.[5] The table above contains the mean differences between the sexes on the self-placement left–right scale in the 1983 and 2001 British Election Study.[6] The mean differences are not substantial. In both studies the majority of respondents placed themselves in the middle of the scale limiting the amount of variation to be explained within any group. However, there is a small but significant difference between the mean values of men and women born between 1947 and 1986 in the 2001 survey, indicating that women respondents born between these years placed themselves slightly to the left of men. The direc-tion of the gaps is in line with the gender generation gap theory in each case, although the other gaps are not statistically significant. Thus, there is some evi-dence to support Norris's gender generation gap thesis, where younger women are predicted to be more left-leaning than younger men. As the results, represented in Table 3.2, provide support for the gender generation gap theory it would be inter-esting to further the investigation by conducting a rigorous time-series analysis of self-placement on the left–right scale. However, the self-placement variable is not available in every BES. The birth cohorts were simplified to two groups to test Pippa Norris's finding that the gender generation gap is evident in post-Second-World-War birth cohorts.

### Socialist/laissez-faire and liberal–authoritarian scales

Self-placement measures of ideology can be problematic because we do not know what respondents understand the left–right scale to be. For such reasons researchers often prefer to calculate ideological position by amalgamating responses to different attitude questions (Sanders 1999).

A set of scales developed by Heath et al. to measure socialist/laissez-faire and liberal–authoritarian ideology are widely used in studies of voting behaviour research (Heath, Evans and Martin 1993). They provide convincing evidence for the robustness of these scales. However, feminist theory and especially gender gap theory suggest that these scales might provoke different responses in the sexes. Heath et al.'s bi-dimensional scales are the most recent advance in a long-running academic debate that proceeded Converse's study of belief systems in mass publics (Converse 1964). Many studies of the gender gap in voting in the United States suggest that women will prioritise healthcare and education spending and that this emphasis can explain why they are more likely to vote for the Democratic candidates in presidential elections than men. Implicit within this argument is the assumption that the indicators of the traditional left–right scale might not ade-quately explain the left-leaning tendencies of women. The hypothesis drawn from this model would be that the traditional left–right scale should not have as large an impact on women's voting as men's but that indicators that specifically address health and education should have greater explanatory power in regard to the voting choice of women. This model is further defined by the introduction of the liberal–authoritarian scale. The research from the United States which supports the argument outlined above contains a parallel dimension, where Southern religious women are more likely to affiliate with the Republican Party, but their motivations are thought to be based in moral conservatism rather than left–right position. This leads us to a second hypothesis, namely, that older and/or religious women's voting behaviour will be better explained by the liberal–authoritarian scale than by the left–right scale.

As well as applying the standard scales, a gender perspective requires us to test the scale for gender dimensions. This will require us to look at each item within the scale and theorise whether there might be gender implications. So, the first step in the analysis is to assess whether the scales are gendered and the second step is to see whether their effect on voting behaviour is different between men and women. The hypotheses considered thus far have been generated by reference to the literature from the United States. The aggregate gender gap evident in the United States is not apparent in Britain, although there is some evidence that this gap might be evident within age groups. It is important therefore to consider the implications of the context. It may be that in Britain factors such as class interact with sex to produce gendered effects within subgroups.

There has been a large body of research responding to Converse's study of belief systems in mass publics (Converse 1964). Converse tested what he described as 'issue constraint'. He compared inter-correlations on issues assuming that high correlation coefficients supported the notion that a single liberal/conservative scale underlay attitude structures. He found a close relationship between different issue preferences in political elites but no such strong correlation was evident in the mass public. In the 1980s there were a spate of articles in which confirmatory factor analysis was used to test whether issues hung together in liberal–conservative scales (Conover 1980; Feldman 1988; Fleishman 1988; Judd, Krosnick and Milburn 1981; Judd and Milburn 1980). The literature suggests that individual's responses to certain issues are related and that it should be possible to predict an individual's attitudes toward, say, nationalisation using their attitudes toward the redistribution of wealth. Possibly, the lack of structure evident in Converse's analysis can be attributed to the fact that values are at least bi-dimensional. In Britain, Heath *et al.* have developed stable and robust liberal–authoritarian and socialist/laissez-faire scales, which support the contention that the belief structures in mass publics, are at least bi-dimensional or are best explained by the use of two scales (Heath, Evans and Martin 1993). Such scales are often employed in studies of voting behaviour in Britain and if gender differences are found within the scales this will impact on our understanding of British electoral behaviour.

An analysis of whether responses to Heath *et al.*'s scales are patterned by gender will be undertaken in the next section. Firstly, the components of the scale will be outlined and discussed. Secondly analysis is undertaken, in Table 3.3, to determine whether Heath *et al.*'s scales are equally applicable to men and women and men and women from different birth cohorts. Finally, the analysis in Table 3.4 attempts to test whether there are substantive gender differences in location on Heath *et al.*'s scales.

In addition to the theories already outlined Jelen *et al.* suggest that women are more liberal than men and that this is not specifically addressed in the literature (Jelen, Thomas and Wilcox 1994). They state that the gender gap is typically the largest on questions of war and peace, environmental and weaker economic issues. They cite Gilligan's model as a possible reason for the higher levels of sympathy for the disadvantaged found among women. They also suggest that there might be a more self-interested motivation because women tend to be more socio-economically disadvantaged than men. However, Jelen *et al.*'s research locates no significant differences on the left–right scale between men and women in the UK, Germany and the Netherlands. Women were found to be more right wing in Italy and France. But they do find a tendency for women to be more 'doveish' in four out of the six countries examined. Economic issues were only significant in Britain and the Netherlands. In the UK these issues were very specific with, for example, women being less likely than men to believe in the importance of trade unions. Dutch women were much less likely than Dutch men to believe that the unemployed were lazy. Overall, women were found to be less likely than men to support nuclear power. Jelen *et al.* question why, when they have found these differences, was there no gender gap in ideology or positioning on the left–right scale? One might suggest in response that the traditional left–right scale might be inadequate here. Jelen *et al.* propose that the left–right scale might mean different things to men and women (Jelen, Thomas and Wilcox 1994). Alternatively, one might theorise that the difference between men and women will be evident within subgroups and not necessarily at an aggregate level. Norris's gender generation gap theory suggests that women should be more left leaning than men in generations born since the Second World War and the reverse should apply to prior generations. This highlights how subgroup differences can cancel each other out at an aggregate level. The analysis in Table 3.4 attempts to test whether the left–right scale means different things to men and women.

**Testing the robustness of Heath *et al.*'s scales by sex**
The items in Heath *et al.*'s socialist/laissez-faire scale are:
- Ordinary people get their fair share of the nation's wealth;
- There is one law for the rich and one for the poor;
- There is no need for strong trade unions to protect employees' working conditions and wages;
- It is government's responsibility to provide a job for everyone who wants one;
- Private enterprise is the best way to solve Britain's economic problems;
- Major public services and industries ought to be in state ownership.

Figure 3.7: Bi-dimensional attitude structure

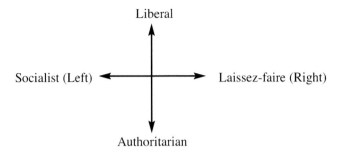

The items in Heath *et al.*'s liberal–authoritarian scale are:

- Young people today don't have enough respect for traditional British values;
- Censorship of films and magazines is necessary to uphold moral standards;
- People in Britain should be more tolerant of those who lead unconventional lives;
- Homosexual relations are always wrong;
- People should be allowed to organise public meetings to protest against the government;
- Even political parties that wish to overthrow democracy should not be banned.

Examination of the items above allows us to make some predictions about how they should apply to the sexes in Britain. If left-leaning ideological positions amongst women are concerned chiefly with the welfare state, we would expect questions about public or private provision of services as well as trade unions to be less significant in their vote choice than those which specifically address education, health and benefits. A scale that is designed to tap into the theoretical priorities of women might contain items such as: 'would you support tax increases for spending on healthcare and/or education?'. A question of this type is available in the 1997 BES.[7] All of the items in Heath *et al.*'s two scales are available in the mail-back component of the 1992 and 1997 BES.[8] The availability of a question that asks respondents to choose reduced taxation or increased government spending on health and social services in the 1997 BES makes it more suitable for this chapter's central research questions and therefore, the 1997 BES is used in all subsequent analysis.

When the six socialist/laissez faire items are summed into a scale, the range of actual scores is 6–28, the mean is 15.3 and the standard deviation is 3.6 (n=2399). The Cronbach's Alpha Coefficient of the scale is 0.67, indicating that it is internally reliable. The Cronbach's Alpha Coefficient for the male respondents was 0.67 and 0.66 for the female respondents. The Cronbach's Alpha Coefficient for those born between 1907 and 1946 was 0.69 for men and 0.68 for women. The Cronbach's Alpha Coefficient for respondents born between 1947 and 1976 was 0.67 for men and 0.63 for women. These figures suggest that the scale was marginally less reliable for the younger women than for the rest of the sample.

Table 3.3: Descriptive statistics and scale reliability for Heath *et al.*'s Socialist/Laissez-Faire and Liberal/Authoritarian scales in the 1997 BES

| Scale | Birth cohort | Sex | Cronbach's Alpha | Mean | Standard deviation | Range |
|---|---|---|---|---|---|---|
| Socialist/ Laissez-Faire | 1907–1946 | Men | 0.69 | 15.4 | 4.2 | 6–27 |
| | | Women | 0.68 | 15.7 | 3.8 | 6–28 |
| | 1947–1976* | Men | 0.67 | 15.5 | 3.7 | 6–28 |
| | | Women | 0.63 | 14.8 | 3.3 | 7–26 |
| | All | Men | 0.67 | 15.4 | 3.7 | 6–28 |
| | | Women | 0.66 | 15.2 | 3.8 | 6–28 |
| | | All | 0.67 | 15.3 | 3.6 | 6–28 |
| Liberal/ Authoritarian | 1907–1946 | Men | 0.52 | 20.3 | 3.3 | 9–30 |
| | | Women | 0.47 | 20.4 | 2.9 | 10–30 |
| | 1947–1976 | Men | 0.62 | 17.9 | 3.6 | 7–27 |
| | | Women | 0.54 | 17.9 | 3.1 | 6–28 |
| | All | Men | 0.62 | 18.9 | 3.6 | 7–30 |
| | | Women | 0.58 | 18.9 | 3.3 | 6–30 |
| | | All | 0.59 | 18.9 | 3.4 | 6–30 |

*The mean difference between the sexes was significant at the 0.01 level.

However, the values are all above 0.6 and therefore are acceptable. The only significant mean difference between the sexes was among the respondents born between 1947 and 1976 where British women were slightly left of men on the scale.

The liberal–authoritarian scale is less reliable than the socialist/laissez-faire scale.[9] The Cronbach's Alpha Coefficient[10] ranged from 0.47 for women born between 1907 and 1946 and 0.62 for all men. The most significant mean differences are between the age groups and not the sexes. Overall, there is little difference between the sexes in Britain in the reliability of either scale, suggesting that they are suitable measures for men and women and different generations of men and women.

There is some evidence to support the gender generation gap thesis since women born after the Second World War were slightly more left-leaning then men of the same generations. Correlation coefficients were calculated between the socialist/laissez-faire scale and the self-placement left–right scale. There were no significant differences between the sexes or sex/generation; hence, the scales are appropriate for both sexes.

The analysis thus far has focused on sex and sex and age or birth cohort. Gender is a term which is designed to capture the relationship of the sex variable to social context. Sex cross-cuts all other demographic factors and women from different groups may not share the same priorities. It is therefore necessary to

Table 3.4: Mean difference in ideological position between the sexes in the 1997 BES

| Sub-group | | Socialist/ Laissez-Faire | Liberal/ Authoritarian |
|---|---|---|---|
| | | Gender gap | Gender gap |
| Age | 18–24 | 0.66 | 0.36 |
| | 25–34 | 0.45 | -0.03 |
| | 35–44 | 0.47 | -0.03 |
| | 45–54 | 0.07 | 0.58** |
| | 55–59 | 0.06 | -0.83 |
| | 60–64 | -0.42 | -0.67 |
| | 65+ | -0.52 | 0.11 |
| Birth cohort | 1967–1976 | 0.71* | -0.38 |
| | 1957–1966 | 0.69* | 0.10 |
| | 1947–1956 | 0.35 | 0.45 |
| | 1937–1946 | -0.52 | -0.29 |
| | 1927–1936 | -0.16 | 0.05 |
| | 1917–1926 | -0.68 | 0.14 |
| Marital status | Married | 0.11 | 0.07 |
| | Not married | 0.16 | -0.17 |
| Education | No qualification | -0.09 | 0.39 |
| | CSE or equivalent | -1.8*** | 0.56 |
| | O Level or equivalent | 0.06 | 0.11 |
| | A Level or equivalent | 1.14*** | 0.01 |
| | Higher education below degree | 0.27 | 0.23 |
| | Degree | 1.66*** | -0.6 |
| Race* | White | 0.09 | -0.08 |
| | Not white | 1.58** | 2.91*** |
| Goldthorpe - Heath class | Working class | -0.44 | 0.45 |
| | Supervisors and manual foreman | -0.14 | -0.56 |
| | Petty Bourgeoisie | -0.39 | 0.02 |
| | Routine non-manual | 0.40 | -1.65*** |
| | Salariat | 0.94*** | 0.14 |
| Household income (quartiles) | Lowest | -0.62 | 0.30 |
| | Second | 0.22 | 0.16 |
| | Third | 0.67** | 0.52 |
| | Highest | 0.56 | -0.21 |
| Religion | C of E / Anglican | -0.09 | -0.06 |
| | Roman Catholic | 0.53 | 1.29*** |
| | Other Christian | 0.31 | 0.37 |
| | Non-Christian | 0.59 | 2.0 |
| | No religion | 0.33 | 0.37 |
| | Total | 0.16 | 0.05 |

*The sample size for these categories was less than 50          **Significant at the 0.05 level
***Significant at the 0.01 level

analyse the measures of ideology by sex within sub-groups. Table 3.4 contains all of the sub-sectors analysed by Pippa Norris[11] in her article on the gender gap in the United States (Norris 2001). The table is replicated here, but instead of examining the gender gap in voting, the mean difference between the sexes' responses to Heath *et al.*'s socialist/laissez-faire and liberal–authoritarian scales are presented. There are no significant differences between men and women's responses to the socialist/laissez-faire scale within age groups but there are significant differences by birth cohort. Women born between 1957 and 1976 are slightly more left-leaning than men of the same generations. Women with a CSE or equivalent are more right-leaning than men with the same qualifications; whilst women with A-levels or a degree are slightly to the left of men with the same qualifications. The evidence suggests that it is possible that education has a different impact on the ideological preferences of men and women. There is a significant difference in the mean position of non-white men and women on the socialist/laissez-faire scale but the small sample size undermines any further extrapolation. Within the salariat, women are slightly more left-leaning than men, indicating that occupational class may also have a different impact on the ideological preferences of men and women. There are some significant mean differences between the sexes within the liberal–authoritarian scale. Roman Catholic women give slightly more liberal responses than Roman Catholic men. There are other significant differences that were not predicted and are not easy to interpret. Notably, women aged 45–54 are slightly more liberal than men of the same age but this pattern was not continued in those over 54. Overall, there is some evidence to support the gender generation gap in left–right position and some evidence to suggest that education and occupational class might interact with sex to produce different ideological positions.

### Alternative measures of ideology

In the introduction to the section on ideology it was mentioned that questions asking respondents to state their position on tax versus spending on welfare provision might be more appropriate measures of the left–right position of women than the traditional measures. A question of this type is available in the 1997 BES. Respondents were asked to choose between one of these three options:

1. Reduce taxes and spend less on health, education and social benefits;
2. Keep taxes and spending on these services at the same level as now;
3. Increase taxes and spend more on health, education and social benefits.

Of the respondents, 73 per cent selected increased taxation and spending, 25 per cent opted to keep taxes and spending at the same level and only 3 per cent of respondents stated that taxes and spending should be reduced. When the data are broken down by sex, 74 per cent of women and 71 per cent of men opted for increased taxation and spending. Of respondents born between 1947 and 1976, 76 per cent of women and 70 per cent of men selected increased taxation and spending. There is therefore a small percentage difference between the two, with 6 per cent more women than men opting for increased taxation and spending on welfare in post-Second-World-War generations. The data are heavily skewed and further analysis is restricted since there is little variation to be explained. The tendency to answer in the affirmative is repeated in questions asking whether more money should be invested in health and education. The response patterns support the contention that ordered questions are the most successful way of accessing issue priority or preference. This is because when asked to respond to a single-issue statement the majority of respondents tend to answer the same way.

Another suggested explanation for the gender generation gap is the rise in post-materialist values. Inglehart's post-materialist theory claims that the generations born since the Second World War have enjoyed more financial security than previous generations and have therefore begun to prioritise non-material political issues, such as reproductive rights, sexual harassment in the workplace and equal opportunities (Inglehart 1977). Norris claims that: 'If this process has influenced the gender gap, support for post-materialist values should be closely associated with left-wing female voting patterns' (Norris 1999: 155). Furthermore, Evans *et al.* note that the post-materialist measurement instrument does not yield clear results (Evans, Heath and Lalljee 1996).

In the most frequently employed version of Inglehart's measure, respondents are asked the question:

If you had to choose from among the items on this card, which are the two that seem most desirable to you?
    Maintaining order in the nation;
    Giving people more say in important political decisions;
    Fighting rising prices;
    Protecting freedom of speech.

People who select 'maintaining order' and 'fighting rising prices' as their two priorities are defined as materialists. People who select 'more say' and 'freedom of speech' are defined as post materialists. The remainder (the majority of the samples) are defined as mixed cases (Evans, Heath and Lalljee 1996: 100).

The measure is available in the 1997 BES. As highlighted by Evans *et al.*, the majority of respondents are described as mixed, with 60 per cent of the valid responses to the 1997 BES falling into this category. Only 30 per cent of respondents could be described as materialist and only 12 per cent fell into the post-materialist category. When the responses were broken down by sex and sex/generation there were no significant differences. The skewed nature of responses to the post-materialist scale seriously limits any explanatory power it might be predicted to have.

Some of the attitudes described by Inglehart as post-materialist are specifically feminist. An alternative to using the post-materialist scale might be to use measures of feminist attitudes. One could use responses to the statement 'equal opportunities for women in Britain have gone too far'.

Bernadette Hayes tested the impact of feminist orientation on vote choice and found that feminist attitudes can be used to predict votes for the Labour Party and

Table 3.5: Responses to whether equal opportunities for women in Britain have gone too far in the 1997 BES (Percentages)

| Group | Sex | Too far | About right | Not far enough | Total* |
|-------|-----|---------|-------------|----------------|--------|
| All | Male | 8.7 | 54.6 | 35.7 | 100 |
| | Female | 9.3 | 42.6 | 46.2 | 100 |
| Born 1907–1946 | Male | 8.6 | 54.5 | 35.3 | 100 |
| | Female | 13 | 46.5 | 37.6 | 100 |
| Born 1947–1976 | Male | 9.2 | 53.3 | 37.1 | 100 |
| | female | 6.9 | 39.2 | 53.4 | 100 |

*The total includes the percentage of missing values.

that these attitudes can be possessed by both men and women and that sex/gender has no direct effect on vote (Hayes 1997). Hayes conducted her analysis on the 1992 BES, using three variables to measure feminist orientations. The first asks whether women are given too few opportunities within political parties, the second whether women should have an equal role with men in running business industry or government and the third, whether equal opportunities for women in Britain have gone too far. The first question is not available in the 1997 BES. This could be problematic because perceptions of parties' attitudes to feminist concerns are cited by Hayes as explaining the link between feminist attitudes and support for the Labour Party.

In Table 3.5[12] the largest gap between the sexes occurs in those respondents who were born after 1947, where 16 per cent more women than men stated that equal opportunities for women had not gone far enough. Hayes found that feminist attitudes predicted Labour Party votes of men and women equally well. Thus, if more younger women than younger men possess feminist attitudes we have a possible explanation of the gender generation gap.

The patterns evident in Table 3.5 are more pronounced in Table 3.6.[13] There was no significant gap between men and women born prior to the Second World War but there was a significant gap between the sexes in the post-Second World War generations, with women agreeing more strongly than men with the statement 'women should have an equal role with men in running business industry or government'.

The analysis in this chapter thus far has considered issue preference in ordered questions, using the 2001 BES and issue-scale location, using the 1997 BES. An alternative method to assess issue preference is to test what measures have the largest effect on vote choice. An attempt to establish whether issues have a differential impact on the vote choices of men and women is complicated by the responses to issue questions. As outlined above, many of the questions of interest tend to provoke affirmative answers in the majority of respondents, limiting their use in regression analysis. However, it is worth attempting some preliminary regression. The logistic regression coefficients, standard errors and Exp(B)s for

Table 3.6: Mean responses to the statement women should have an equal role with men in running business industry or government or women should stay in the home

| Group | Gender gap or mean difference |
|---|---|
| All | 0.26* |
| Born 1907–1946 | 0.04 |
| Born 1947–1976 | 0.40* |

*Significant at the 0.01 level, Anova one-tailed test.

six logistic regressions are presented in Table 3.7.

The dependent variable is vote choice; whether the respondent claimed to have voted for the Conservative or the Labour Party.[14] The first regression was conducted on men only and the second on women only and the results are reported in the section entitled Group/All of Table 3.7. The third and fourth regressions were conducted on respondents who were born between 1907 and 1946, analysing men and women separately. Two regressions were conducted on respondents born between 1947 and 1976, also analysing men and women separately. Post-materialism did not have any significant effects on vote within any of the groups analysed other than women born between 1947 and 1976, where, contrary to theory, post-materialism increased the likelihood of voting for the Conservative Party. The findings may be the result of the ineffectiveness of the measure employed. In all of the generations, the tax/spend on welfare variable had a larger impact on the vote choice of women than men. In the whole sample, women who chose increased taxation and spending on welfare were 5½ times more likely to vote for the Labour Party than those who didn't, whilst men who chose increased taxation and spending on welfare were 2½ times more likely to vote for the Labour Party than those who didn't. Amongst the respondents born between 1907 and 1946, women who chose taxation were eight times more likely to vote for the Labour Party than those who didn't and men who chose taxation were four times more likely to vote for the Labour Party than those who didn't. In the group born between 1947 and 1976 the tax and spend question did not have a significant effect on the vote choices of men, but had a significant effect on the vote choice of women, with women who choose taxation 5½ times as likely to vote for Labour than those who did not.[15]

The socialist/laissez-faire and self-placement left/right position scales had roughly the same effect on the vote choices of men and women in all groups. The gender differences in the impact of the tax/spend variable on vote supports the contention that welfare provision is likely to be especially important to women. Among the respondents born between 1947 and 1976 the liberal–authoritarian scale had a significant effect on the vote choice of men but not women. With each step up the authoritarian scale men became 15 per cent less likely to vote for the Labour Party. The significance of the relationship between liberal–authoritarian position and vote amongst men was not predicted by feminist theory or gender gap theory. The effect is echoed by the number of young male respondents who prioritised asylum or

Table 3.7: Logistic regression on vote in the 1997 General Election

| Group | Independent variables | Sex | B | S.E. | Exp(B) |
|---|---|---|---|---|---|
| All<br><br>n=956 | Post-materialism | Male | 0.518 | 0.775 | 1.678 |
| | | Female | -0.863 | 0.729 | 0.422 |
| | Liberal/Authoritarian | Male | -0.099** | 0.049 | 0.905 |
| | | Female | -0.131** | 0.059 | 0.878 |
| | Socialist/Laissez-Faire | Male | -0.395*** | 0.055 | 0.673 |
| | | Female | -0.518*** | 0.073 | 0.596 |
| | Self-placement Left/Right | Male | -0.511*** | 0.099 | 0.600 |
| | | Female | -0.817*** | 0.122 | 0.442 |
| | Taxes and spending on welfare | Male | 0.924*** | 0.345 | 2.521 |
| | | Female | 1.729*** | 0.447 | 5.634 |
| | Equal opportunities for women scale | Male | -0.074 | 0.319 | 0.929 |
| | | Female | 0.416 | 0.361 | 1.516 |
| Born between 1907 and 1946<br><br>n=428 | Post-materialism | Male | -0.298 | 1.285 | 0.743 |
| | | Female | 0.175 | 1.191 | 1.191 |
| | Liberal/Authoritarian | Male | -0.055 | 0.074 | 0.946 |
| | | Female | -0.117 | 0.108 | 0.890 |
| | Socialist/Laissez-Faire | Male | -0.432*** | 0.083 | 0.649 |
| | | Female | -0.454*** | 0.108 | 0.635 |
| | Self-placement Left/Right | Male | -0.556*** | 0.154 | 0.573 |
| | | Female | -0.784*** | 0.166 | 0.457 |
| | Taxes and spending on welfare | Male | 1.415** | 0.530 | 4.116 |
| | | Female | 2.084** | 0.731 | 8.038 |
| | Equal opportunities for women scale | Male | -0.842 | 0.525 | 0.431 |
| | | Female | -0.329 | 0.574 | 0.719 |
| Born between 1947 and 1976<br><br>n=507 | Post-materialism | Male | 0.763 | 1.020 | 2.145 |
| | | Female | -2.025** | 1.027 | 0.132 |
| | Liberal/Authoritarian | Male | -0.166* | 0.071 | 0.847 |
| | | Female | -0.122 | 0.080 | 0.885 |
| | Socialist/Laissez-Faire | Male | -0.362*** | 0.078 | 0.696 |
| | | Female | -0.611*** | 0.117 | 0.543 |
| | Self-placement Left/Right | Male | -0.653*** | 0.158 | 0.521 |
| | | Female | -0.983*** | 0.203 | 0.374 |
| | Taxes and spending on welfare | Male | 0.569 | 0.492 | 1.776 |
| | | Female | 1.725** | 0.682 | 5.611 |
| | Equal opportunities for women scale | Male | 0.230 | 0.436 | 3.272 |
| | | Female | 1.185** | 0.548 | 1.338 |

*Significant at the 0.10 level
**Significant at the 0.05 level
***Significant at the 0.01 level

immigration in the 2001 general election and warrants further investigation. The measure of feminist orientation employed had a significant effect on the vote choice of women born between 1947 and 1976. Women who felt that equal opportunities for women in Britain had not gone far enough were 34 per cent more likely to vote for the Labour Party than those women who did not.[16]

## SUMMARY

The research presented in this chapter has demonstrated that there are differences between men and women (and especially different generations of men and women) in issue preference and location. It is apparent from analysis of the 2001 BES that women are more likely to prioritise education and healthcare issues and men are more likely to select the economy as their most important election issue. The differences between the sexes are most interesting when they are broken down by age, with younger women more likely to prioritise education and older women more likely to prioritise healthcare. Men aged between fifty-five and fifty-nine were twice as likely than the rest of the sample to be most concerned about the European Union. These sub-group differences highlight the necessity of integrating the study of sex differences with other demographic factors, to avoid making essentialist claims about the nature of the sexes and to analyse rigorously the impact of the sex variable on political attitudes. The sex difference in issue priority presented in this chapter provides support for Anne Phillips's claims for gender quotas in Britain because there is evidence that men and women might want slightly different things from the political system and these differences need to be represented.

There is evidence in the 1997 and 2001 British Election Studies to support the existence of an ideological gender generation gap, which underpins Norris's gender generation gap theory of vote choice. Women born after the Second World War were significantly to the left of men on the self-placement left–right scale. Women born after 1957 were significantly more left-leaning on Heath *et al.*'s socialist/laissez-faire scale than men. The two findings support Norris and Inglehart's modern gender gap theory (Inglehart and Norris 2000).

No evidence was found that Heath *et al.*'s measures of ideology were less valid for women, or women of different generations, than men. This study has demonstrated that women born after the Second World War in Britain are significantly more feminist than men of the same generations and this has a significant effect on vote choice. No evidence was found to suggest that post-materialist values affected the vote choices of men and women in different ways. However, such insignificant effects may be a result of the weakness of the measurement instruments used and some more analysis with questions designed specifically for this task would be helpful.

The analysis in this chapter has been descriptive and not causal, but there is some evidence to suggest that education and occupation might have different effects on the ideological position of men and women. Women who had A-levels or a degree were significantly more left-leaning than men with the same qualifications. Female members of the salariat were also more left-leaning than male members.

The scope of this chapter is limited by its dependency on secondary data analysis. The questions used where not designed for the study's purpose and were not available in a continuous time series. The lack of key information, for example whether the respondent was a mother, prohibits a thorough investigation of whether feminist standpoint theory, rational choice theory or an 'ethics of care' can provide the best account of the gender differences outlined in this chapter. The gender differences in issue preference and ideology presented here suggest evidence of women's interests that are distinct from men's in small but significant areas.

## NOTES

1   This chapter was first published as 'Gender, ideology and issue preference: is there such a thing as a political women's interest in Britain?' in the *British Journal of Politics and International Relations* 2004, 6: 20–46, and was republished in Hill, L. and Chappell, L., (eds), 2005, *The Politics of Women's Interests: New Comparative Perspectives*, Routledge: London. I would like to express my thanks to Blackwell for permitting republication. I am extremely grateful to Joni Lovenduski and Peter John for all their comments and support and to all those who commented upon earlier versions of this chapter.

2   The British Election Study has been conducted since 1964. The 2001 study was funded by the ESRC and directed by David Sanders and Paul Whiteley, of the University of Essex, and Harold Clarke and Marianne Stewart from the University of Texas at Dallas.

3   BES 2001 cross-section variable name=bisssum Most Important Issue-Summary

4   There is a sharp increase in the number of respondents reporting pensions as the most important election issue for the over 65s. In order to gain more detailed information about respondents' issue preferences it would be useful to ask them for a number of key election issues.

5   In this case, the gender gap is the mean value of the male responses minus the mean value of the female responses. The significance of the difference is calculated using ANOVA.

6   The self-placement on the left–right scale was coded 0 left to 10 right. This was recoded –5 left, 0 middle and 5 Right. The 1963, 1964 and 1966 British Election Studies asked respondents about their location on the left–right scale. First a filter question was asked: 'Do you ever think of yourself as being to the left, the centre, or the right in politics, or don't you think of yourself that way?' In 1963 68 per cent of respondents stated that they 'did not see themselves that way'. This figure was 62.4 per cent in the 1964 survey and 64.6 per cent in the 1966 survey. In each of these studies those respondents who replied to the filter question in the affirmative were then asked to place themselves on the left–right scale. The low response rate to the filter question means that any further analysis of the self-selection left–right variable will be seriously undermined because there is unlikely to be a representative sample of responses to the question. This low response rate may also be an indictment

of forced self-selection left-right questions, where respondents are asked to place themselves on a scale without an opt out. These findings reinforce the strategy utilised in this chapter where left–right position is measured by a battery of items and tested for internal reliability and compared to self-placement on the left–right scale. In the 1970, 1974 Feb & Oct, 1979, 1987, 1992 &1997 BES respondents were not asked to place themselves on the left–right scale. In the 1983, 1997 and 2001 BES the self-placement left–right scale question was asked without a filter. In 1983 valid responses were coded from −10 for left to +10 for right and 87.9 per cent of the respondents answered this question. In 2001 valid responses were coded from 0 left and 10 right and 83.2 per cent of respondents answered the question.

7   It would be preferable to test this over time but the item required is only available in the 1997 BES.

8   Half of the scales are coded in reverse order i.e. from right to left instead of left to right. In order to create a scale these items are reversed.

9   This lower reliability is reported by Heath *et al.*

10  The Cronbach's Alpha test for reliability was used by Heath *et al.* and its use here permits a replication of Heath *et al.* The replication is followed by tests to establish whether the scales are equally reliable when applied to men and women and different groups of men and women.

11  The components of Norris's table are included here because it permits us to examine whether the sub-group sex difference found in the US by Norris are evident in Britain.

12  Respondents were asked whether they thought equal opportunities for women in Britain had gone too far. They could respond 'much too far', 'too far', 'about right', 'not far enough' or 'not nearly far enough'. 'Much too far' and 'too far' were recoded as 'too far' and 'not far enough' and 'not nearly far enough' were coded together as 'not far enough'.

13  Respondents were asked to place themselves on a 11-point scale from A: 'women should have an equal role' to K: 'women's place is in the home'. The majority of respondents placed themselves in one of the first three categories A–C.

14  Vote was coded 1 for Labour and 0 for Conservative.

15  Interaction terms suggest that the difference between the sexes is insignificant, with a significance level of 0.08. However, cross tabulations suggests that there is a bivariate relationship.

16  Whole sample: Men Nagelkerke $R^2 = 0.622$. Women Nagelkerke $R^2 = 0.770$. Older respondents: Men Nagelkerke $R^2 = 0.672$. Women Nagelkerke $R^2 = 0.752$. Younger respondents: Men Nagelkerke $R^2 = 0.618$. Women Nagelkerke $R^2 = 0.798$.

# chapter four | gender and turnout

The study of turnout is an important component of studies of political participation but it should also be incorporated into models of voting behaviour, 'even if the abstention was not intended, it is part of the behaviour of voters on election day and should be covered in analysis' (Catt 1996: 67). Evidentially, not voting is one option available to electors and might be described as one category in a dependent variable that would also contain party of vote. It is particularly important to consider the potential interactions between gender and voter turnout because they may cause gendered patterns in party choice. This chapter proceeds by describing the changing pattern of gender and turnout over time. It then moves to consider whether gender differences in voter turnout impact upon any gender gap in vote choice or party preferences.

Analyses of gender and turnout tend to be included within the broader political participation literature. Historically, women have been less likely than men to participate in formal politics, including voting in elections. There is still a gender gap in political activity but in recent years the gender gap in turnout has declined and even reversed so that women are now slightly more likely than men to vote: the trend is illustrated in Figure 4.1. The turnout gap, however, is not statistically significant and tends to disappear when age is controlled for (Norris, Lovenduski, and Campbell 2004).

The modest gender gap in turnout presented in Figure 4.1 is based upon self-reported turnout. In recent years the BES team have checked self-reported figures with constituency records in order to remove misreporting. Table 4.1 compares self-reported and verified turnout in the 1992, 1997 and 2001 general elections.

Overall, between 1992 and 2001, women were marginally more likely to vote than men in each election. It would seem that the largest difference between self-reported and verified turnout is evident in the 2001 BES for both sexes, the relationship between sex and vote is not affected by verification. We can conclude that there is a modest but statistically insignificant gender gap in turnout in Britain. Thus, there is very little relationship between sex and voter participation. However, before moving on from the analysis of turnout to party of vote it is necessary to ensure that any gender differences in voting behaviour are not attributable to different levels of misreporting of turnout. For example, it is possible that a gender gap whereby more

Figure 4.1: Electoral turnout by sex, 1964–2001[1]

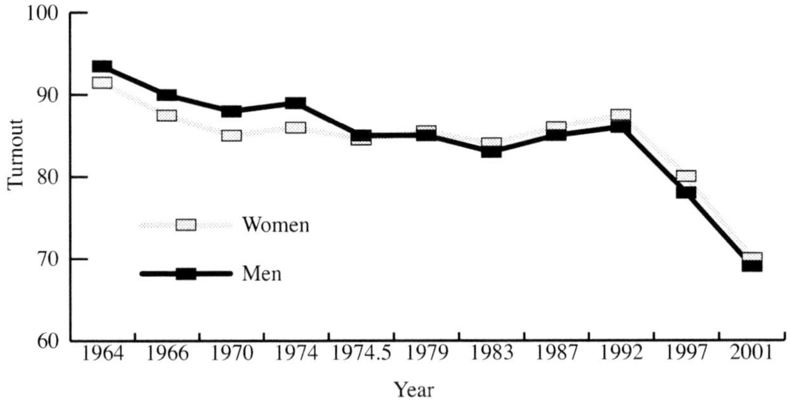

Source, the BES series.

Table 4.1: Respondent's turnout, self reported and verified, in the 2001, 1997 and 1992 British election studies, by sex

| Sex | Vote | 2001 | | | 1997 | | | 1992 | | |
|---|---|---|---|---|---|---|---|---|---|---|
| | | Voted | Didn't vote | Total | Voted | Didn't vote | Total | Voted | Didn't vote | Total |
| Male | Self-reported | 66.8% | 31.1% | 100% | 77.9% | 22.1% | 100% | 86.8% | 13.1% | 100% |
| | Verified | 63.0% | 37.0% | 100% | 73.7% | 26.3% | 100% | 84.7% | 15.3% | 100% |
| Female | Self-reported | 69.9% | 30.1% | 100% | 79.5% | 20.5% | 100% | 88.1% | 11.8% | 100% |
| | Verified | 64.6% | 35.4% | 100% | 75.0% | 25.0% | 100% | 85.9% | 85.9% | 100% |

Table 4.2: The gender gap by age group, 1992–2001[2], verified and non-verified voters[3]

| Year | Under 25* | | Aged 25–44 | | Aged 45–65 | | Aged 65+ | |
|---|---|---|---|---|---|---|---|---|
| | Self-stated voters | Verified voters only | Self-stated voters | Verified voters only | Self-stated voters | Verified voters only | Self-stated voters | Verified voters only |
| 1992 | 31 | 38 | -7 | -8 | -6 | -6 | -17 | -15 |
| 1997 | 15 | -3 | 9 | 9 | -10 | -12 | -15 | -17 |
| 2001 | -20 | -16 | 11 | 14 | -12 | -14 | -10 | -4 |

* The cell counts in this age range tend to be very small.

young women than young men seem to vote for the Labour Party could be attributable to lower turnout among Labour supporting young men.

Table 4.2 illustrates the gender gap within age groups in the 1992, 1997 and 2001 BESs. The gaps are calculated first for all respondents who claimed to have voted and second for respondents whose vote was verified by the research team.[4]

The difference between the self-stated and verified gender gap figures is most profound in the under-twenty-fives in the 1997 BES, where the self-stated gap is fifteen points and the verified gap is −3 points.[5] In the 2001 general election, the gender generation gap reversed in the under-twenty-fives whichever measure was employed. The data suggest several possibilities. Firstly that young, Labour-supporting women may have been more likely not to turn out in the 2001 election. Secondly, that the gender gap is reverting to tradition within this age group. Alternatively the difference may be a blip evident only in this dataset. The differences found in Table 4.2 demonstrate that it is preferable to use verified voting data when analysing gender gaps. It should be noted that using verified votes is not cost free; it will exclude some misreporting at the cost of losing some valid data. It will not exclude all misreporting, because some respondents who did vote may not have voted for the party that they stated. In 1997 the Labour party received 44.4 per cent of the vote. However, according to the 1997 BES, 49.1 per cent of respondents claimed to have voted for the Labour Party. When non-verified voters were excluded, 48.4 per cent of the respondents claimed to have voted Labour. The overstatement, or over-representation, of Labour votes was accompanied by the under-reporting, or under-representation, of Conservative votes and a representative sample of Liberal Democrat voters; the verification procedure only reduced this bias marginally.

## GENDER AND TURNOUT IN THE 2001 GENERAL ELECTION

The 2001 British general election provides a useful case study for examining the relationship between gender and turnout. Electoral turnout declined from 71.4 per cent in 1997 to 59.5 per cent in 2001. The dramatic fall in voting levels spurred a renewed interest in the study of non-voting in Britain. This section attempts to establish whether explanations of non-voting developed in 2001 require a gender dimension and whether turnout effects influence gender differences in party of vote.

### Is the gender gap a product of sex differences in turnout?
Table 4.2 suggests that the gender generation gap was evident in the twenty-five to forty-four age group but was not evident among the youngest respondents to the 2001 BES. Before we can analyse gender and party of vote in more detail it is necessary to establish whether turnout effects impacted upon the gender differences in party of vote displayed in Table 4.2. One way of testing whether the gender gap in party of vote is an artefact of a gender gap in turnout is to check if a gender gap is evident in attitudes to political parties. If the reversal in the gender generation gap in vote in 2001 can be explained by a gender generation gap in turnout, then we would expect to find that more women under twenty-five than men under twenty-five identified with Labour, but that fewer Labour-supporting young women voted.

However, when the partisan gender gap is calculated for age groups it becomes apparent that the absence of a modern gender gap in the under-twenty-fives is not

Table 4.3: Partisan identification by sex and age group in the 2001 BES

| Age group | Partisan gender gap 2001 |
|-----------|--------------------------|
| 18–24 | 0.6 |
| 25–44 | 13.2 |
| 45–64 | –6.7 |
| 65+ | –12 |
| All | –1 |

n=2508

simply a feature of the reduced turnout in 2001. The number of respondents in the under-twenty-five category is 216, which is too small to make generalisations about the wider population. However the modern gender generation gap is evident among the twenty-five to forty-four year olds, irrespective of turnout effects and the sample size for this group is 989, which is large enough for us to make generalisations about the electorate. The gender generation gap will be considered in more detail in the next chapter. This chapter has established that the gender generation gap is not an artefact of turnout effects.

**Turnout at the 2001 general election: was there a gender dimension?**
There was not a statistically significant gender gap in turnout in the 2001 general election, according to the BES verified vote figures, 63 per cent of men and 64 per cent of women voted. Table 4.4 demonstrates that the only significant gender gap in turnout within age groups was evident among respondents aged between forty-five and sixty-four, where women were 6 per cent more likely to vote than men. Overall, younger women were slightly less likely to vote than younger men and older women were slightly more likely to vote than older men but these differences are marginal.

Although there was not a gender gap in turnout in the 2001 general election it

Table 4.4: Validated turnout by age-grouped and sex, from the 2001 BES

| Sex | Age group | Voted | Didn't Vote | Total |
|-----|-----------|-------|-------------|-------|
| Male | Under 25 | 41.7% | 58.3% | 100% |
| | 25–44 | 56.3% | 43.7% | 100% |
| | 45–64* | 70.4% | 29.6% | 100% |
| | 65+ | 78.4.% | 21.6% | 100% |
| | Total | 63.0% | 37.0% | 100% |
| Female | Under 25 | 38.8% | 61.2% | 100% |
| | 25–44 | 54.4% | 45.6% | 100% |
| | 45–64 | 76.5% | 23.5% | 100% |
| | 65+ | 78.3% | 21.7% | 100% |
| | Total | 64.6% | 35.4% | 100% |

* The difference between the sexes was significant at the 0.05 level, chi-square test. n=2823

is possible that there may have been a motivational gender gap. A motivational gender gap would occur if men and women choose to vote for different reasons. Research published on turnout in the 2001 general election has demonstrated marginality or the closeness of the race is one of the best predictors of turnout and that turnout was at its lowest in safe Labour seats (Berrington 2001; Harrop 2001; Whiteley *et al.* 2001). The analysis below is not intended to challenge these findings. Rather it is intended to demonstrate that background factors can interact with more immediate factors, such as interest in politics. Sociological variables may not produce dramatic changes in electoral behaviour independently but they can interact with the specific context of an election to produce differential effects. The failure of sociological factors to provide a complete explanation of electoral change is demonstrated by Whiteley *et al.* They point out that the decline in voter turnout between 1997 and 2001 cannot be explained by purely sociological factors 'since the variables at the centre of such accounts like social class, education, ethnicity and gender do not change enough in four years to provide an adequate explanation of what occurred' (Whiteley *et al.* 2001: 212). However, we have seen in Chapter three and in previous sections of this chapter that there is a relationship between sex, age and political attitudes and that there are gender gaps in vote within age groups. Thus, it is possible that sex and age had an impact on the intermediary variables, such as interest in politics, and therefore had an indirect effect on turnout.

Some theories of gender difference suggest that women are likely to be more disaffected by the media representation of politics as a spectator sport[6] (Stephenson 1998). There is also a suggestion that women are more likely to be floating voters than men. During the 2001 election polling data indicated that a Labour win was inevitable (Crewe 2001). The Conservative Party fought a poor campaign and the media coverage concentrated on the campaign rather than the issues. There are now two conflicting hypotheses. The first suggests that young women will be more likely to vote for the Labour Party because it might be thought the party that will best represent their hypothesised preference for spending on social services. The second leads to the prediction that women might be less likely to vote than men in the specific context of the 2001 general election. During the 1997 British general election the Fawcett Society conducted focus groups with women before and after the election, 'and after the election they said that they switched off, or did not read coverage of the election. These women often described themselves as not interested in politics, but during discussion groups, as they discussed deeply held concerns and opinions about the future of the health and education service, changes in the job market, local, national and European government proposals and how they might affect their lives, it became clear that it was the way politics was presented rather than the issues themselves that they were not interested in'(Stephenson 1998). Their report goes on to claim that women do not relate to the presentation of elections in the media as a spectator sport and that they are less tolerant to evidence of 'sleaze' in politics. Pippa Norris's developmental theory of the gender gap suggests that as education and full-time employment outside the home increases women will become more left-wing. Research from the United States suggests that women's left-wing ideology will be related to specific issues such as spending on education and health. Uniting these models it is possible to generate a hypothesis relating to the 2001 general election.

*H1: Women who would have voted for the Labour Party in 2001 did not vote because they felt that the Labour Party had not delivered in the policy areas most important to them, namely education and health.*

In order to test the hypothesis a structural equation model of turnout is developed and applied to men and women of different ages separately. The coefficients adjacent to the paths can be interpreted in the same manner as standardised regression coefficients in OLS regression. In Figures 4.2 and 4.3 the model is applied to men and women under the age of thirty-five. The model is applied to the under-thirty-fives because it is within this group that the general trend, where marginally more women than men vote, is reversed in the 2001 BES.

Figures 4:2 and 4:3 represent a structural model of turnout amongst women and men under thirty-five in the 2001 BES. The chi-square is 47 with 27 degrees of freedom, which can be interpreted as a good fit on the rule-of-thumb basis that the chi-square should not be more than twice as large as the degrees of freedom. The male sample size is 501 and the female sample is 528. The models are not

Figure 4:2: Model of turnout in the 2001 general election. Male respondents under 35. (Standardised solution)

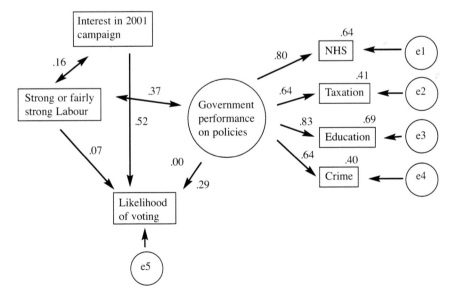

Figure 4:3: Model of turnout in the 2001 general election. Female respondents under 35. (Standardised solution)

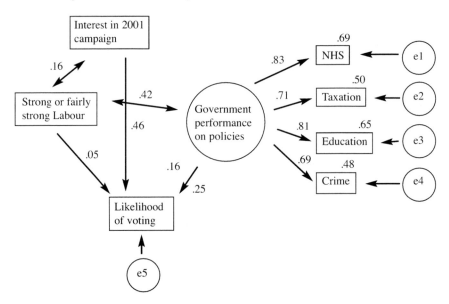

intended to provide comprehensive explanations of turnout but are designed to highlight different relationships amongst the variables between the sexes. In the male sample the latent variable government performance on policy does not have a significant effect on likelihood of voting. In the female sample, the factor-loading/regression weight is 0.16, significant at the 0.01 per cent level. Hence, female respondents who viewed Labour's policy performance positively were more likely to vote than those who did not, which was not true of men under thirty-five. The coefficients between 'strong' or 'fairly strong' Labour supporters were not significant in either the male or female sample. When all age ranges were considered, the strong or fairly strong Labour Party identification was not significant in the female sample but was significant in the male sample; the standardised regression coefficient was 0.08, suggesting a weak relationship. Government performance on policies was not significant in the male sample but was significant in the female sample; the standardised regression coefficient was 0.1, indicating a stronger relationship.

Altogether, these models provide tentative evidence that, in the under thirty-fives, assessment of government performance on policies had a stronger effect on turnout amongst women than men. It also suggests that strong or fairly strong Labour Party identity had had a larger effect on men in the sample than women.

It would appear that evaluations of government policy performance have a stronger effect on the turnout of younger women than men. In the case of the 2001 election the reversal in the gender generation gap in turnout can, in part, be accounted for by young women's dissatisfaction with the Labour government's

Figure 4.4: Path model of likelihood of voting, under 35s only

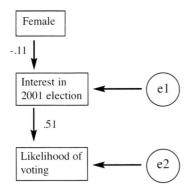

Chi-square = 5.330
Degrees of freedom = 1
Probability level = 0.021
Both of the standardised regression coefficients are significant at the 99 per cent level.

policy performance and young men's tendency to be more influenced by a sense of party loyalty. However, the strongest predictor of vote amongst all groups is interest in politics. Interest in politics is patterned by sex.

The modification indices suggest that model would be slightly improved if an arrow was drawn between sex and likelihood of voting. However, this would mean that the model was just identified or that the ratio of unknown to known parameters was too high to compare model fit but the coefficient was 0.06. The output suggests that interest in the 2001 election explains some of the variation in likelihood of turnout by sex but not all of it. When the only variables in the model are sex and likelihood of voting there is not a significant relationship. The indirect effect of sex on likelihood of voting is found by multiplying the two regression coefficients together. In this case –0.11 x 0.51 = –0.06. which indicates a small direct effect of sex on likelihood of voting in this model.

**Logistic regression model of turnout in the 2001 general election**
Principal components analysis (rotated) was used to create four variables; political cynicism, interest in politics and two policy performance variables. Cynicism in politics was created using three items: MPs lose touch with people, parties are only interested in votes and government does not care.[7] Interest in politics was calculated using respondent's attention to politics, interest in politics and their interest in the 2001 election.[8] The policy performance variables were divided into two. The first contained the respondents' performance evaluations of the Labour government on the NHS, education and pensions and the second contained performance on the economy, taxation and inflation. The policy performance indicators were not combined into one scale because the correlation coefficients were too low.[9] When two separate scales were used, 65 per cent of the variance was

Table 4:5: Logistic regression of turnout in 2001

| Independent variables | Turned out | | |
|---|---|---|---|
| | b | SE(b) | Exp(b) |
| Cynicism in politics | 0.46 | 0.06 | 1.05 |
| Interest in politics | -0.72 | 0.06*** | 0.49 |
| Knowledge about politics | 0.21 | 0.05*** | 1.24 |
| Strong/fairly strong Labour party identification | 0.18 | 0.13 | 1.19 |
| No party can handle most important issue | -0.01 | 0.15 | 0.99 |
| Social Class | -0.01 | 0.04 | 0.98 |
| Labour government handle NHS and Education | -0.11 | 0.06* | 0.89 |
| Labour government handle economy, inflation and taxation | 0.00 | 0.06 | 1.00 |
| Age grouped | 0.20 | 0.03*** | 1.22 |
| Female | 0.70 | 0.12*** | 2.02 |
| Female under 35 | -0.70 | 0.18*** | 0.50 |
| Constant | -0.84 | 0.30** | 0.43 |

* 90 per cent level ** 95 per cent level *** 99 per cent level
2-log likelihood 2483
per cent of cases correctly classified 76.8
n = 2497

explained by the first principal factor.

The results above indicate that those who were not interested in politics were less likely to vote than those who were, and that those who were knowledgeable about politics were more likely to vote than those who weren't. It also supports the previous evidence, which indicates that, overall, women were more likely to vote than men but that women under thirty-five were less likely to vote than the rest of the sample. However, when the model is applied to the under-thirty-fives, sex becomes insignificant. When a binary logistic regression is applied to turnout in the under-thirty-fives and sex is the only independent variable it is significant at the 99 per cent level, with an Exp(b) of 0.685. These results suggest that the differential turnout between young men and young women can be explained with reference to the variables in the model. Differential levels of interest or knowledge about politics produced a lower turnout in young women. The simple structural model presented in Figure 12 allows us to calculate what the indirect effect of sex on likelihood of voting through interest in the 2001 election might be.

The preliminary analysis presented in this section indicates that the 2001 election results were gendered in several different ways. Pippa Norris's gender generation gap holds true among the over-twenty-fives, but in the under-twenty-fives more women voted for the Conservative Party than men. The models presented in this section demonstrate that assessments of government policy performance may have had a stronger effect upon the turnout of younger women than younger men. It also suggests that younger women were less interested in the 2001 general election than younger men and that this suppressed turnout; these findings demonstrate that theoretically driven models of gender difference must be integrated with analysis of the specific electoral context in order to provide comprehensive models of gender and vote. These findings contribute to general models of turnout because they demonstrate that sex has a small indirect effect on turnout mediated by other factors. However, gender differences are not static and background influences such as sex impact upon electoral specific factors to influence turnout.

## SUMMARY

This chapter has demonstrated that it is preferable to use verified turnout statistics when analysing voting behaviour. The need for verified statistics is particularly important when looking at gender gaps, which tend to be only very small percentage-point differences. It has been established that the gender generation gap evident in post-war generations is not merely a product of turnout differences. The analysis of potential motivational gender gaps in turnout at the 2001 British general election have shown that, overall, the closeness of the election and other aggregate level variables are far better predictors of turnout than the sex variable; but sex does have a small indirect effect on turnout, mitigated by other factors such as interest in politics and other election-specific factors. The analysis in the last section is exploratory and serves to highlight possible underlying gendered effects.

## NOTES

1    All of the figures are self-stated turnout rates and not validated turnout because the verification data is not available for the whole series.

2    At the time of writing, the verified figures for the 2005 BES were not available.

3    This is a reproduction of Table 8.3 (Norris 1999: 156), with the addition of the verified voters column. The 1963–87 BESs were not included because they do not contain a verified/validated vote variable. Respondents who claimed not to have voted were excluded from both columns. The gender gap was calculated by (per cent female respondents who voted Labour – per cent female respondents who voted Conservative) – (per cent male respondents who voted Labour – per cent male respondents who voted Conservative.)

4    The team who produce the British Election Study collect data to verify whether respondents voted, they cannot ascertain who respondents voted for but they can establish whether they voted at all. This verification process was undertaken for the 1992, 1997 and 2001 studies but not for any previous studies; the analysis is therefore limited to these three elections.

5    In all three studies, 1992, 1997 and 2001, the under-twenty-fives make up a small component of the sample and many of the cell frequencies are very small; therefore any extrapolation from differences within this age group to the wider population is likely to be unreliable.

6    Stephenson, M. (1998). *The Glass Trapdoor: Women, Politics and the Media in the 1997 General Election*, Fawcett: London. This research was only conducted on women, which limits the scope of the conclusions that we can draw from it as it is not possible to say that

women were any different to men. However, it does help us to generate some useful hypotheses about the 2001 general election.

7   These variables were Likert scales: code 1 strongly agree to 5 strongly disagree. The principal component explained 71 per cent of the variance and the eigenvalue was 2.15; all of the factor loadings were above 0.8.

8   The principal component explained 75.5 per cent of the variance and the eigenvalue was 2.27; all of the factor loadings were above 0.8.

9   The principal component for a scale which contained crime, taxation, education and the NHS only explained 53 per cent of the variance and the eigenvalue was 2.2; all but one of the factor loadings were below 0.8. When education and NHS were included in one scale, the first principal component explained 75 per cent of the variance but the eigenvalue was 1.5; the factor loadings were both over 0.8. The second scale contained the economy, taxation and inflation: the first principal component explained 64 per cent of the variance, the eigenvalue was 1.92 and the factor loadings were 0.86, 0.82 and 0.7.

# chapter five | sex, vote and other background characteristics

## INTRODUCTION

This chapter moves on from attitudes and turnout and considers the interactions between sex and other background characteristics. As outlined in the introduction, this book utilises the funnel of causality to conceptualise the indirect effects sex might have upon political behaviour through other factors. Most of the background characteristics that are included in models of political behaviour, such as class, income and education, have a gender dimension. In Chapter three we saw how sex influences attitudes, which in turn might influence vote choice. In this chapter we consider the relationships between gender and parenthood, occupational class, income, marital status and education and whether they impact upon vote choice.

This chapter helps us to employ a concept of gender rather than simply adding in the sex variable. Thinking about gender requires an understanding of how sex interacts with other background characteristics. As outlined in Chapter one, it is very common to include the sex variable as a control in models of voting behaviour. However, this approach very often washes out important gender effects. For example, the modern and traditional gender gaps are evident within age groups but not at an aggregate level. Thus, we must endeavour to understand how background characteristics such as sex and age, sex and class or sex and race[1] interact and how this might impact upon political behaviour.

This chapter will proceed by analysing the gender gap within subgroups. Finally a model of gender, background characteristics and vote is presented.

## GENDERING BACKGROUND CHARACTERISTICS

As explained in Chapter one, feminist theories provide insight into the impact of mothering upon the psychologies of the sexes (Chodorow 1978; Gilligan 1982; Ruddick 1989). Such theories suggest that women are less likely to develop a separate sense of self than men or that they are more likely to conceptualise justice or equity through relationships rather than abstract principles. Women might, therefore, prioritise increased taxation even if they are not the direct beneficiaries. This is said to be because the socialisation of girls encourages them to place emphasis on the interest of others. Alternative explanations of gender differences in behaviour posit the different lived experiences of men and women as the cause of different personal preferences. Thus, a self-interested rather than altruistic motivation might operate. A rational choice explanation of gender difference must be based upon different interests and thus preferences between the sexes. In contemporary Western democracies, women are now much more likely to participate in the paid workforce and to be highly educated than previous generations of women. However, women continue to undertake the majority of unpaid caring and domestic work. Hence, the different life experiences of the sexes might yield different sets of political preferences and perceived self-interests. Women who are mothers may be more likely to vote for parties that they believe will improve the state provision of care for their children, such as quality education and healthcare programmes. Alternatively, men who are more likely to work full-time and to undertake less childcare may perceive that their interests are best served by reducing tax payments and allowing them to take a larger proportion of their wage home. If these differences in the burden of care account for the gender generation gap, then we would expect women with children to be more likely to vote for the Labour Party, while it is promising increased spending on health and education, than men with children. However, the test is muddied because women who do not have children may vote for parties on the basis of their anticipated future interests. Furthermore, it is likely that the sexual division of labour in the workplace, as well as the sexual division of labour in the home, has an impact upon vote choice. Women have not entered paid employment in all areas in equal numbers to men and women are more likely than men to be employed in the public sector.[2] A fact that may provide at least a partial explanation for leftward shift in the attitudes of younger women. This chapter will therefore consider the impact of motherhood and public sector employment on partisan identification (used as a proxy for vote choice).

As discussed previously, it is very difficult to disentangle altruistic from self-interested motivations from hypotheses about women's political behaviour being more 'other-related' than men's. This chapter should help to separate the two motivations by assessing whether motherhood or other background characteristics explain gender differences or whether it persists after such controls are added. Should adding such controls demonstrate that the gender gap persists irrespective of whether women have children or not, we would have weak evidence of the 'ethics of care' motivation for behaviour.

### Analysis

The analysis undertaken in this chapter is conducted on an amalgamated dataset created by combining the 2001 and 2002 British Social Attitude Surveys (BSA).[3] The BSA was selected in place of the British Election Study Series (BES) because a number of years can be combined together to provide a large sample of data collected over a short time period. The 2001 and 2002 combined dataset has 6722 respondents.[4] A large dataset is particularly helpful here because Norris's gender generation gap theory predicts that differences between men and women will vary by birth cohort, requiring sufficient numbers of respondents in each group to compare the sexes. The BSA also includes a measure of parenthood and caring for dependent children, which is not available in the BES series and is a crucial component of the models of gender difference. Unfortunately, the BSA does not include a vote or a validated vote[5] variable and partisan identification is used as a proxy for party of vote in the analysis.

Figures 5.1 to 5.3 illustrate the patterns of partisan identification by sex and birth cohort using the 2000, 2001 and 2002 BSAs. Overall there is more similarity than difference and men and women follow approximately the same trends. However, the minor differences are worth exploring because of their potential impact upon election outcomes. It has been claimed that, had women voted Labour in equal numbers to men, then Britain would have had consecutive Labour governments since 1945 (Harmen and Mattinson 2000). However, although marginal percentage point differences can influence election outcomes we should be careful not to exaggerate the differences between the sexes. As mentioned previously, even in the United States, where an aggregate gender gap has been evident since 1980, many commentators and researchers have stressed the narrowness of the gap (Greenberg 2001; Kaufmann and Petrocik 1999; Seltzer, Newman and Leighton 1997). Richard Seltzer *et al.* note that 'in 1994, women voted 7 to 11 percentage points more Democratic than men…and the race gap between whites and

Figure 5.1: Conservative partisan identification by birth cohort and sex, from the 2000–02 British Social Attitudes Survey

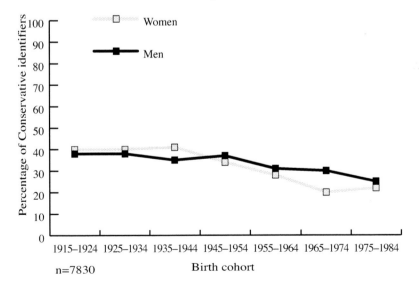

n=7830

Figure 5.2: Labour partisan identification, by birth cohort and sex, from the 2000–02 British Social Attitudes Survey

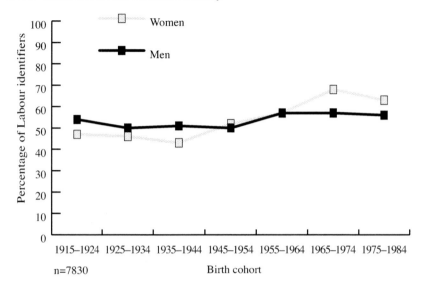

Figure 5.3: Liberal Democrat partisan identification, by birth cohort and sex, from the 2000–02 British Social Attitudes Survey

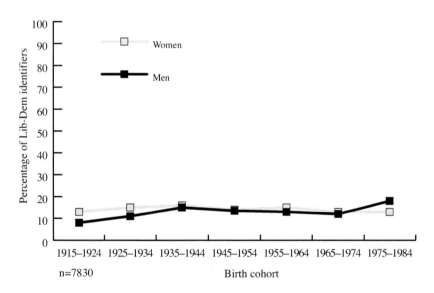

blacks was a true chasm of 50 points'. In response to these tensions, this research attempts to understand gender as a background characteristic that might combine with other factors to influence election outcomes rather than overemphasising small differences between women and men in general.

Examination of Figures 5.1 to 5.3 demonstrates that the historic tendency for women to be more likely to identify with the Conservative Party than men was not evident amongst respondents born after 1945. Women in the younger generational cohorts were slightly more likely than men to identify with the Labour Party. Women were marginally more likely to identify with the Liberal Democrats than men in every group except those born after 1974. The figures clearly illustrate that sex is not a good indicator of party support. In fact the only statistically significant gap between the sexes support for the Conservative Party was evident amongst those born between 1965 and 1974, where men were 6.5 per cent more likely than women to be Conservative identifiers. There were two statistically significant gaps between the sexes' support for the Labour Party. Amongst respondents born between 1935 and 1944, men were 8 per cent more likely than women to identify with the Labour Party. Women respondents born between 1965 and 1974 were 7 per cent more likely than men of the same generation to identify with the Labour Party. The only statistically significant sex difference evident within Liberal Democrat support is amongst respondents born between 1975 and 1984, where men were 5 per cent more likely than women to be Liberal Democrat identifiers. These small gaps illustrate that there is some minimal difference between the sexes' affiliation to the parties, that may influence election outcomes.

The analysis presented in Figures 5.1 to 5.3 corroborates findings from the 2001 BES which revealed no evidence of the gender generation gap amongst the youngest respondents, but showed a statistically significant gap between those born between 1945 and 1976.

There is some evidence of small differences between the sexes in support for the parties by generation. The gender gap in the US is calculated by subtracting votes for the Republican Party from votes for the Democrat Party. However, such a two-party approach is no longer appropriate in Britain, which, at the national level, is at least a three-party system. Therefore the analysis will proceed by comparing all three main parties.

The simple descriptive statistics presented thus far illustrate that there is some limited evidence of the gender generation gap. The analysis will now move to consider whether motivational gender gaps exist in vote choice.[6]

Table 5.1 examines the relationship between three background characteristics and sex and vote. Overall older men were more likely to vote Labour than Liberal Democrat and older women were more likely to vote Conservative than Labour. Men and women with children were more likely to vote Labour than Liberal Democrat. Married men were more likely to vote Lib Dem. Married men and women were both more likely to vote Conservative than Labour. Women with children of their own under eleven years old living within the household were more likely to vote Labour than Conservative. In order to check the validity of the results the regression was repeated on the whole sample of men and women together, when an interaction term for women with children is included the overall effect of having children disappears and the women with children variable is

Table 5.1: The impact of age, marital status and parenthood on partisan identification by sex[7]

| Partisan identification | Independent variable | Sex | B | Std. Error | Sig. | Exp(B) |
|---|---|---|---|---|---|---|
| Labour/ Conservative | Age | Men | -.750 | .161 | .122 | 1.005 |
| | | Women | -1.745*** | .140 | .000 | 1.020 |
| | Married | Men | -.437*** | .103 | .000 | .646 |
| | | Women | -.415*** | .088 | .000 | .660 |
| | Children under 11 | Men | .173 | .134 | .197 | 1.189 |
| | | Women | .419** | .124 | .001 | 1.521 |
| Labour/ Liberal Democrat | Age | Men | -.012** | .004 | .002 | .988 |
| | | Women | -.002 | .003 | .540 | .998 |
| | Married | Men | -.269* | .135 | .047 | .764 |
| | | Women | -.156 | .110 | .157 | .856 |
| | Children under 11 | Men | .714*** | .185 | .000 | 2.043 |
| | | Women | .589*** | .147 | .000 | 1.803 |

n=5255

statistically significant at the 0.001 level with an exp(B) of 1.7, indicating that women with children were 70 per cent more likely to support the Labour Party than the rest of the sample. It would appear that having children under eleven had a significant impact upon the Labour/Conservative vote of women and not men. This finding is consistent with feminist theories of gender difference that suggest that the impact of mothering has an important impact on the psychology of the sexes.

In order to be absolutely certain that the impact of parenthood on party identification demonstrated in Table 5.1 is not an age effect, the respondents' partisan identification for those aged between twenty-five and forty-four was calculated and is presented in Table 5.2.

There was a 20-point gender gap between men and women and men aged twenty-five to forty-five with children of their own under eleven in the home, where women were more likely to support the Labour Party and less likely to support the Conservative Party than men; this difference was significant at the 0.001 level (chi-square test). There was a 7.1-point gender gap between men and women

Table 5.2: The partisan identification of respondents aged between 25 and 44 by parenthood and sex

| Parent | Sex | Party identification | | | |
|---|---|---|---|---|---|
| | | Conservative | Labour | Lib Dem | Total |
| Parent of child under 11 in home | Men | 30.7% | 58.4% | 10.9% | 100% |
| | Women | 20.0% | 67.7% | 12.3% | 100% |
| | Total | 24.2% | 64.1% | 11.8% | 100% |
| Not parent of child under 11 | Men | 25.6% | 55.8% | 18.6% | 100% |
| | Women | 21.3% | 58.3% | 20.3% | 100% |
| | Total | 23.5% | 57.1% | 19.5% | 100% |

aged twenty-five to forty-five without children under eleven in the home but the difference was not statistically significant. Overall, respondents with children were 5 per cent more likely to identify with the Labour Party than respondents without children. The difference between mothers and the rest of the respondents was small but statistically significant.

Table 5.3: The relationship between Labour/Conservative partisan identification and background characteristics

| Partisan identification | Independent variables | Sex | Exp (B) | SE |
|---|---|---|---|---|
| Labour/ Conservative | Age | Men | 1.01 | 0.005 |
| | | Women | 1.04*** | 0.005 |
| | Married | Men | 0.81 | 0.169 |
| | | Women | 0.90 | 0.133 |
| | Parent of child under eleven | Men | 1.42 | 0.216 |
| | | Women | 1.21 | 0.183 |
| | Salariat[8] | Men | 2.99*** | 0.214 |
| | | Women | 1.35 | 0.217 |
| | Routine non-manual | Men | 2.00* | 0.279 |
| | | Women | 1.55** | 0.167 |
| | Manual foremen and supervisors | Men | 1.46 | 0.244 |
| | | Women | 1.65 | 0.360 |
| | Degree[9] | Men | 1.25 | 0.318 |
| | | Women | 1.69 | 0.292 |
| | Higher education below degree | Men | 1.64 | 0.290 |
| | | Women | 1.97** | 0.254 |
| | A levels or equivalent | Men | 2.54** | 0.279 |
| | | Women | 3.02*** | 0.254 |
| | O levels or equivalent | Men | 2.25** | 0.266 |
| | | Women | 3.08*** | 0.211 |
| | CSE or equivalent | Men | 1.66 | 0.274 |
| | | Women | 2.44*** | 0.236 |
| | Low income | Men | 1.41* | 0.168 |
| | | Women | 2.40*** | 0.144 |
| | Voluntary sector employment[10] | Men | 1.13 | 0.527 |
| | | Women | 0.45* | 0.393 |
| | Public industry employment | Men | 0.93 | 0.363 |
| | | Women | 0.90 | 0.578 |
| | Public sector employment | Men | 0.72 | 0.202 |
| | | Women | 0.71* | 0.145 |
| | Psuedo $R^2$ (Cox and Snell) | Men | 0.109 | |
| | | Women | 0.126 | |

n for men = 1081 n for women = 1526      ***Differences significant at the 0.001 level
**Differences significant at the 0.01 level      * Differences significant at the 0.05 level

Tables 5.1 and 5.2 demonstrate that women with children were more likely to vote for the Labour Party than the rest of the sample. Age had a significant impact upon the Conservative/Labour support of women and not men, this is consistent with the gender generation gap thesis. Married men and women were both more likely to support the Conservative Party than the Labour Party even after controlling for age. Tables 5.3 and 5.4 repeat the regression presented in Table 5.1 but also includes education, occupational class, public sector employment and income. After the inclusion of these variables, the impact of marriage and children upon Conservative/Labour partisan identification disappears.

Age had a significant impact upon the Labour/Conservative support among women and not among men.[11] Older women were more likely to support the Conservative Party than younger women and this difference between old and young was more profound amongst women than men. This finding supports the gender generation gap thesis that younger generations of women are moving to the left. The occupational class, income and educational attainment variables had a similar impact upon the Conservative/Labour party choice of men and women. However, being a member of the salariat had a stronger impact upon men; whilst being employed in the public sector had a stronger impact upon women. The regression was repeated, adding each of the three new variables individually. The relationship between Conservative/Labour Party support and having children disappeared when household income was controlled for, suggesting that the effect is only evident within particular income groups.

It is difficult to operationalise theories of gender difference when considering Labour/Liberal Democrat party support. The literature tends to focus on Conservative/Labour support and it is not known whether the public perceive the Labour or Liberal Democrat party as more likely to prioritise spending on health and education. Men and women with children under eleven were more likely to vote for the Labour Party than the Liberal Democrats. Men and women with degrees were also more likely to vote for the Liberal Democrats than the Labour party. The sex differences were marginal and not predicted by theory.

The most significant finding of Tables 5.3 and 5.4 is that, after household income is included as a control, being the parent of a child under eleven in the home no longer has a significant impact upon the Conservative/Labour party identification of women. Table 5.5 considers the relationship between Conservative/Labour party support, sex and income to establish whether the gender generation gap can be attributed to sex differences within the sub-group of respondents who are both parents and middle/high income earners.

The only statistically significant difference between the sexes occurs amongst respondents with middle or high incomes who are parents of children under eleven in the home. Women in this group were 10 per cent more likely to support the Labour party than men. In the middle/high income group individuals who were not parents of children under eleven living in their home, men were marginally more likely than women to support the Labour Party. There was no difference in party support between men and women without children in the low-income group,

Table 5.4: The relationship between Labour/Liberal Democrat partisan identification and background characteristics

| Partisan identification | Independent variables | Sex | Exp (B) | SE |
|---|---|---|---|---|
| Labour/ Liberal Democrat | Age | Men | 0.99 | 0.007 |
| | | Women | 1.01* | 0.006 |
| | Married | Men | 0.80 | 0.211 |
| | | Women | 0.89 | 0.158 |
| | Parent of child under eleven | Men | 1.87* | 0.278 |
| | | Women | 1.58* | 0.207 |
| | Salariat | Men | 1.11 | 0.274 |
| | | Women | 1.35 | 0.264 |
| | Routine non-manual | Men | 1.44 | 0.320 |
| | | Women | 1.51* | 0.203 |
| | Manual foremen and supervisors | Men | 0.95 | 0.319 |
| | | Women | 2.09 | 0.392 |
| | Degree | Men | 2.24* | 0.373 |
| | | Women | 3.54*** | 0.319 |
| | Higher education below degree | Men | 1.95* | 0.344 |
| | | Women | 1.77 | 0.312 |
| | A levels or equivalent | Men | 1.52 | 0.346 |
| | | Women | 1.67 | 0.326 |
| | O levels or equivalent | Men | 0.94 | 0.361 |
| | | Women | 2.54*** | 0.255 |
| | CSE or equivalent | Men | 0.756 | 0.383 |
| | | Women | 2.25*** | 0.284 |
| | Low income | Men | 1.29 | 0.208 |
| | | Women | 1.17 | 0.171 |
| | Voluntary sector employment | Men | 1.16 | 0.627 |
| | | Women | 0.84 | 0.405 |
| | Public industry employment | Men | 0.91 | 0.467 |
| | | Women | 2.05 | 0.528 |
| | Public sector employment | Men | 1.21 | 0.226 |
| | | Women | 0.926 | 0.169 |
| | Psuedo $R^2$ | Men | 0.109 | |
| | | Women | 0.126 | |

n for men = 1081 n for women = 1526     ***Differences significant at the 0.001 level
**Differences significant at the 0.01 level    *Differences significant at the 0.05 level

where more than 70 per cent of both sexes were Labour Party rather than Conservative Party supporters. There was a 9 per cent difference in Labour Party support among low-income parents but it was not statistically significant. Overall, mothers were more likely to support the Labour Party than fathers and middle/high income mothers were significantly more likely to support the Labour Party than middle/high income fathers. These findings suggest that the rational

Table 5.5: Conservative/Labour party identification by sex and household income

| Household income | Parent of child in home | Sex | Party support | | Total |
|---|---|---|---|---|---|
| | | | Conservative | Labour | |
| Middle/high[12] | Not a parent | Men | 41.6% | 58.4% | 100% |
| | | Women | 44.1% | 55.9% | 100% |
| | Parent of child under 11* | Men | 41.8% | 58.2% | 100% |
| | | Women | 31.9% | 68.1% | 100% |
| Low | Not a parent | Men | 27.3% | 72.7% | 100% |
| | | Women | 28.5% | 71.5% | 100% |
| | Parent of child under 11 | Men | 22.5% | 77.5% | 100% |
| | | Women | 13.8% | 86.2% | 100% |

n=2199
*Difference between the sexes significant at the 0.05 level, chi-square test

choice or feminist standpoint explanations of the gender gap might provide better explanations than the ethics of care, because the main difference is between men and women who are middle- or high-income earners, where mothers may have a preference for better education and healthcare provision and men may prefer lower taxes. However, it is possible that the lack of difference between the party support of the low-income groups hides underlying motivational differences. Women may support the Labour Party because of its perceived emphasis on health and education and low-income men may believe that the Labour Party will best support their own financial interests. We can conclude, however, that the Labour Party has successfully obtained the support of middle/high income mothers to a greater degree than middle/high income fathers.

## CONCLUSION

This chapter has demonstrated that background factors interact to produce effects on voting behaviour and party support. Age has a more profound effect on the Labour/Conservative support of women than men. Occupation had a slightly different impact upon the vote choice of men and women. Being a member of the salariat was a better predictor of men's decision to vote Conservative than women's and being employed in the public sector was a better explanation of women's choice to vote Labour than men's. Education and income both have similar impacts upon the party support of women and men, but household income interacts with sex and parenthood to influence party support. Younger women were more likely to support the Labour party than younger men and mothers were more likely to support the labour party than fathers. However, the difference in Labour Party support between mothers and fathers is only significant within middle and high income groups. Thus, the relationship between sex, other background characteristics and vote is complex and it is likely that the effect of the interactions at election time will be mediated by issue salience. The Labour Party has successfully portrayed itself as the party of health and education in recent years and this may have led the underlying motivational gender gap to produce gender differences in vote choice. The relationship between gender, vote and electoral context will be examined in the following chapters.

## NOTES

1   Interactions between sex and race are not included in the analysis because of sample-size issues.
2   In the combined 2001 and 2002 BSA, 75 per cent of men and 61 per cent of women were employed in the private sector, 4 per cent of men and 1 per cent of women were employed in nationalised industries, 19 per cent of men and 34 per cent of women were employed in the public sector and 2 per cent of men and 3 per cent of women were employed in the voluntary or charity sector. The differences between the sexes were significant at the 0.001 level (chi-square test).
3   The BSA survey was conducted by the National Centre for Social Research (NatCen).
4   Only the 2001 and 2002 datasets were amalgamated because the other years did not contain all of the questions of interest.
5   The BES includes a validated vote variable that records whether any given respondent participated in the election.
6   Analysis in the rest of the chapter is conducted on the 2001 and 2002 BSA surveys because the dependent children questions (hhch04, hhch511, hhch1215, hhch1617, rch04, rch511, rch1215 and rch1617) were not asked in the 2000 survey.
7   Cox and Snell pseudo-$R^2$ 0.021 for men and 0.047 for women.
8   The reference category for the occupational class categories is working-class. When public sector employment and occupational class were in the same model petty bourgeoisie coefficients were not calculated. Exploratory analysis was undertaken that showed that this was likely to be due to sample-size issues. The regressions were rerun with public-sector employment and occupational class in different models and the effects were approximately the same as presented here. Tests for multicollinearity were undertaken and there was no evidence of a problem.
9   The reference category for highest educational qualification is no-qualification.
10  The reference category for public sector employment is private-sector employment.
11  The finding was corroborated by including an interaction term for women and age into a regression on the whole sample of men and women; the interaction had significant impact on party support.
12  Middle and high incomes were combined because only a very small number of respondents reported having high incomes.

# chapter six | electoral context

## INTRODUCTION

The models outlined in Chapters three to five were generic models of gender and vote. The generic model of gender and vote contains variables from two of the causal blocks specified by Bartle: social characteristics and stable predispositions (Bartle 1998). A comprehensive model of gender and vote must consider two further blocks: policy preferences and evaluations. Policy preferences have been analysed in some depth in Chapter three. However, attitudes to the economy and economic issues as well as evaluations of leaders and parties have been absent from the previous analysis. Therefore, this chapter on electoral context will proceed with an analysis of gender and economic attitudes and gender and evaluations of parties and leaders.

## ECONOMIC VOTING

A number of articles concerning the gender gap in the United States suggest that economic variables, included in models of voting behaviour, may have different impacts upon the voting choice of men and women. Chaney *et al.* state that one of the key determinates of the gender gap in voting behaviour is the difference in men's and women's perception of economic issues (Chaney, Alvarez and Nagler 1998). Women, they propose, are most interested in the national economic situation, whilst men are more concerned with their personal economic circumstances (Chaney, Alvarez and Nagler 1998: 318). Chaney *et al.* conclude that the gender gap can be explained with an amalgamation of the theories they tested. They suggest that women's less secure position within the economy combines with their compassion to motivate women to vote Democrat. They claim that the only significant issue which men and women politicise differently is the economy, and not more commonly cited 'women's issues' (Chaney, Alvarez and Nagler 1998). Susan Welch and John Hibbing also claim that men are more likely than women to 'vote with their pocket books' and therefore may be inclined to identify with the Republicans (Welch and Hibbing 1992). In the analysis of presidential elections in the US, Harold Clarke *et al.* suggest that the gender gap may be driven by differences in economic expectations (Clarke *et al.* 2004). They discovered that 'women's economic evaluations are consistently more pessimistic than men's' (Clarke *et al.* 2004: 31), and that 'a national prospective economic evaluation model performs best for women, but a personal prospective model works best for men' (Clarke *et al.* 2004: 3).

The theoretical literature predicts that women and men should differ on economic issues and the empirical literature from the United States demonstrates that they do. The results of this research can be extended to consideration of the British case. Do British men and women weigh economic issues differently? Are British women more pessimistic about the economy and more likely to be concerned with the national economy than British men? Finally, if these differences are evident in Britain do they translate into differences in voting behaviour?

A number of influential studies of voting behaviour in Britain have focused on economic explanations (Sanders 1991; Sanders 1996; Sanders *et al.* 2001; Sanders, Ward and Marsh 1991). David Sanders has demonstrated that voters' economic perceptions have influenced vote choice in recent British general elections. However, Helena Catt has suggested that there might be a gender dimension to economic models of voting (Catt 1996). She claims that 'Särlvik and Crewe or Himmelweit, adopted rational choice ideas based on perceptions of "economic man"' (Catt 1996: 9). Thus she is critical of economic theories of voting behaviour for being androcentric. So far, descriptive analysis, presented in Chapter three, has demonstrated that men were more likely than women to select the economy as their most important election issue in the 2001 BES. Theories of gender difference and Catt's critique of mainstream approaches to economic voting suggest that men might be more likely to prioritise taxation and the economy when voting than women. These hypotheses will be tested later in this chapter.

Compassion or 'ethics of care' arguments predict that women will be less likely to be 'pocket book' oriented than men. However, there is an additional aspect to the relationship between gender and economic voting caused by women's relative financial disadvantage. According to a recent Equal Opportunities Commission report women are 6 per cent more likely than men to live in households with incomes that are 60 per cent below the national average (Bradshaw *et al.* 2003). Furthermore almost half of all women have total individual incomes of less than £100 a week, compared with less than a fifth of men (Bradshaw *et al.* 2003). Women's relative poverty has multiple causes. There is a gender wage gap in Britain and in 2002 women working full-time earned 81 per cent of full-time working men's earnings (Social-Trends 2002). The pay gap itself is caused by a number of factors including the gender segregation of work, career breaks for maternity leave – and other caring responsibilities – and unequal pay for equal work. In addition to the gender pay gap, women's disproportionate levels of poverty are caused by the large number of older women living alone on inadequate pensions, low employment rates amongst lone parents (who are overwhelmingly women) and because of unequal distributions of income within households

(Bradshaw *et al*. 2003). These factors lead us to expect that any measure of household income employed in models of voting will have an interaction with the sex variable. The following section will use the 2001 BES[1] to establish whether women and men tend to respond differently to questions pertaining to the national economy and to their personal financial circumstances and whether any such differences remain after household income is controlled for.

There were significant sex differences between the responses to all of the national, personal, prospective and retrospective measures in the 2001 BES. However, most of the differences are attributable to women answering 'stayed the same'– in the middle column – more than men. Men were slightly more likely than women to say that their personal economic circumstances had got both better and worse, women were more likely to say that their circumstances had stayed the same. Women were very slightly more pessimistic about the state of the national economy over the previous year. Overall, 27 per cent of women and 25 per cent of men thought that the national economy had deteriorated over the past year, although 5 per cent more women than men thought that the economy had stayed the same. Men were more likely than women to expect their personal financial circumstances to get both better and worse. The only real difference in national prospective evaluations was that 4 per cent more women then men expected the economy to stay the same. The pattern evident in Table 6.1 is that women were more likely than men to place themselves in the middle (no change) category. The

Table 6.1: National and personal, prospective and retrospective economic evaluations by sex (2001 BES)

| Economic evaluation | Sex | Response | | | | | Total (n) |
|---|---|---|---|---|---|---|---|
| | | Lot worse | Little worse | Stayed the same | Little better | Lot better | |
| Personal perspective[2] | Men** | 5.9% | 18.2% | 42.7% | 26.5% | 6.7% | 100% (1449) |
| | Women | 4.9% | 15.1% | 49.5% | 25.0% | 5.6% | 100% (1535) |
| National perspective[3] | Men** | 3.5% | 21.8% | 35.4% | 35.2% | 4.2% | 100% (1428) |
| | Women | 4.2% | 23.0% | 40.8% | 28.8% | 3.2% | 100% (1451) |
| Personal perspective[4] | Men*** | 2.3% | 18.9% | 46.2% | 27.9% | 4.6% | 100% (1407) |
| | Women | 2.2% | 13.8% | 54.1% | 26.7% | 3.2% | 100% (1478) |
| National perspective[5] | Men* | 4.8% | 30.3% | 36.2% | 26.5% | 2.2% | 100% (1387) |
| | Women | 4.5% | 25.8% | 40.6% | 27.7% | 1.4% | 100% (1398) |

***Difference between the sexes significant at the 0.001 level (chi-square)
**Differences between the sexes significant at the 0.01 level (chi-square)
*Differences between the sexes significant at the 0.05 level (chi-square)

Table 6.2: Feelings about the national economy by sex (2001 BES)

| Feelings about the national economy | Sex | Applies | Doesn't apply | Total (n) |
|---|---|---|---|---|
| Angry | Men** | 18.8% | 81.2% | 100% (1433) |
| | Women | 23.3% | 76.7% | 100% (1491) |
| Happy | Men*** | 43.0% | 57.0% | 100% (1415) |
| | Women | 32.0% | 68.0% | 100% (1473) |
| Disgusted | Men*** | 13.3% | 86.6% | 100% (1436) |
| | Women | 18.2% | 81.8% | 100% (1493) |
| Hopeful | Men | 75.2% | 24.8% | 100% (1432) |
| | Women | 73.0% | 27.0% | 100% (1503) |
| Uneasy | Men | 44.5% | 55.5% | 100% (1430) |
| | Women | 46.0% | 54.0% | 100% (1482) |
| Confident | Men*** | 40.4% | 59.6% | 100% (1428) |
| | Women | 30.8% | 69.2% | 100% (1472) |
| Afraid | Men*** | 14.7% | 85.3% | 100% (1432) |
| | Women | 19.5% | 18.5% | 100% (1490) |
| Proud | Men*** | 29.7% | 70.3% | 100% (1408) |
| | Women | 20.9% | 79.1% | 100% (1460) |

***Difference between the sexes significant at the 0.001 level (chi-square)
**Differences between the sexes significant at the 0.01 level (chi-square)
*Differences between the sexes significant at the 0.05 level (chi-square)

tendency for women to be more likely than men to choose a neutral answer has been established in the political knowledge literature. A large proportion of the difference in the political knowledge scores of men and women can be accounted for by women selecting the middle value or don't know response. Jeffery Mondak and Mary Anderson found that the gender gap in political knowledge was reduced considerably when the neutral value was excluded from the range of potential answers (Mondak and Anderson 2004). The 2001 BES contains a number of measures of feelings towards the economy that do not include a neutral response, allowing us to assess whether any gender differences persist when a forced response is required. Men and women's feelings about the national economy and their own financial circumstances are compared in Tables 6.2 and 6.3.

Overall, the evidence presented in Table 6.2 suggests that when women are forced to make a positive or negative response they are more pessimistic about the national economy than men. Women were more likely than men to say that they felt angry, disgusted or afraid when thinking about the national economy. The largest differences in the sexes' feelings about the economy were apparent when pride, happiness and confidence were measured. Overall, 11 per cent more men than women reported feeling happy about the economy, 10 per cent more men felt confident than women and 9 per cent more men felt proud about the economy than women. We therefore find evidence that women in Britain, like women in the

Table 6.3: Feelings about personal financial circumstances by sex (2001 BES)

| Feelings about personal financial circumstances | Sex | Applies | Doesn't apply | Total (n) |
|---|---|---|---|---|
| Angry | Men* | 14.0% | 86.0% | 100% (1435) |
| | Women | 17.0% | 83.0% | 100% (1532) |
| Happy | Men** | 55.6% | 44.4% | 100% (1427) |
| | Women | 50.2% | 49.8% | 100% (1525) |
| Disgusted | Men* | 10.2% | 89.8% | 100% (1436) |
| | Women | 12.2% | 87.8% | 100% (1527) |
| Hopeful | Men* | 79.1% | 20.9% | 100% (1431) |
| | Women | 75.5% | 24.5% | 100% (1530) |
| Uneasy | Men | 31.2% | 68.8% | 100% (1433) |
| | Women | 30.7% | 69.3% | 100% (1528) |
| Confident | Men** | 55.6% | 44.4% | 100% (1432) |
| | Women | 49.8% | 50.2% | 100% (1513) |
| Afraid | Men** | 12.9% | 87.1% | 100% (1437) |
| | Women | 16.4% | 83.6% | 100% (1527) |
| Proud | Men* | 39.5% | 60.5% | 100% (1422) |
| | Women | 35.4% | 64.6% | 100% (1501) |

***Difference between the sexes significant at the 0.001 level (chi-square)
**Differences between the sexes significant at the 0.01 level (chi-square)
*Differences between the sexes significant at the 0.05 level (chi-square)

United States, are more pessimistic about the national economy than men.

The sex differences in Table 6.3 are less profound than those evident in Table 6.2. The sex differences in feelings about personal financial circumstances are weaker than feelings about the national economy. Men were 5 per cent more likely than women to say that they felt happy about their personal finances and 6 per cent more likely to say that they felt confident about their personal financial situation.

The following section tests whether the sex differences found in feelings about the national economy and personal finances are caused by women's economic disadvantage in society. Factor analyses were conducted on the items listed in Tables 6.2 and 6.3 and regressions were conducted on the resulting latent variables. The factor analyses produced four component factors, measuring positive national economic feelings, negative national economic feelings, positive personal financial feelings and negative personal financial feelings. The factor scores were saved and used as dependent variables in regression models. ANOVA tests were conducted on the factor scores to establish whether there was a mean difference in the responses of men and women. There were significant sex differences in the mean scores of men and women's responses to the positive variables (where the positively phrased feelings, such as happy, confident and proud, had the highest factor scores). Women were less likely than men to claim to have positive feelings about either national or personal economic circumstances. Regressions were then

Table 6.4: OLS regression of positive feelings about the economy and personal financial circumstances (2001 BES)[6]

| Independent variables | Positive national economic feelings | | | | | |
|---|---|---|---|---|---|---|
| | Model 1 | | Model 2 | | Model 3 | |
| | B | SE | B | SE | B | SE |
| Sex | 0.22*** | 0.04 | 0.23*** | 0.05 | 0.22*** | 0.05 |
| Household income | | | 0.022** | 0.01 | -0.002 | 0.01 |
| Occupational class | | | | | -0.04* | 0.02 |
| Education | | | | | 0.03 | 0.02 |
| Age | | | | | -0.001 | 0.02 |
| $R^2$ | 0.012 | | 0.016 | | 0.024 | |
| n | 2681 | | 2022 | | 1924 | |

***Difference between the sexes significant at the 0.001 level
**Differences between the sexes significant at the 0.01 level

| Independent variables | Positive personal economic feelings | | | | | |
|---|---|---|---|---|---|---|
| | Model 1 | | Model 2 | | Model 3 | |
| | B | SE | B | SE | B | SE |
| Sex | -0.11** | 0.03 | 0.09 | 0.05 | 0.08 | 0.05 |
| Household income | | | -0.03*** | | -0.05*** | 0.01 |
| Occupational class | | | | | -0.05** | 0.16 |
| Education | | | | | 0.04* | 0.02 |
| Age | | | | | 3E-05* | 0.001 |
| $R^2$ | 0.003 | | 0.013 | | 0.025 | |
| n | 2832 | | 2121 | | 2016 | |

*Differences between the sexes significant at the 0.05 level
(The VIF scores indicated that multicollinearity does not undermine the models.)

conducted on the positive factor scores and are presented in Table 6.4.

All of the models presented in Table 6.4 have low $R^2$ values and the independent variables explain very little of the variation in feelings about the economy or personal economic feelings. However, the models serve to illustrate the relationship between gender and economic evaluations. The effect of the sex variable upon positive national economic feelings persists and remains fairly constant after household income, occupational class, education and age are controlled for. It would seem that women's relative pessimism about the national economy is not simply a function of their lower socio-economic status. Women, it appears are on average less likely than men to have positive feelings about the national economy. This finding is in keeping with the literature from the United States, outlined in the introduction to this chapter. The impact of the sex variable upon feelings about personal financial circumstances disappears when household income is controlled for. Women's relative dissatisfaction with their own personal financial circumstances, therefore, is a consequence of their average lower incomes. The results of the second regression on personal financial circumstances demonstrates that taking the 'add-women and stir' approach to gender and voting behaviour can overlook important sex differences because, when sex is simply added as a control in models two and three, the differences between the sexes are obscured. Women's relative poverty means that they have, on average, more negative perceptions of their own personal financial circumstances than men, and this may affect their political attitudes. The underlying causes of men and women's poverty are different and models of political behaviour should attempt to incorporate these background relationships if they are to have explanatory power over time, because, should parties target measures at relieving women's burden of care or challenging the gender pay gap, a motivational gender gap may develop. Lower income voters are not a homogenous group, background factors such as sex and ethnicity have an impact upon rates and types of poverty and should be incorporated into models in order to understand the underlying motivations for political behaviour. Having established that British women were more pessimistic about the economy in 2001 than British men we can move on to consider whether they weighed economic issues differently when voting.

Multinomial regressions were conducted with party of vote (Conservative, Labour or Liberal Democrat) as the dependent variable. The regressions were conducted on men and women separately. Retrospective and prospective evaluations of the national economy and personal financial circumstances had a significant effect on the Labour/Conservative vote of men and women. Retrospective and prospective evaluations of the national economy had a significant effect on the Labour/Liberal Democrat vote of men and women but retrospective and prospective evaluations of personal financial circumstances did not affect the Labour/Liberal Democrat vote of either men or women. The regression was repeated but the evaluation variables were replaced with positive feeling variables. In all cases, positive feelings about the national economy had a significant effect on vote choice but positive feelings about personal financial circumstances did not. There were no significant differences between the sexes and no differences were found when interaction terms were used in place of the separate regressions.

This section on gender and economic voting has established that women in Britain are more pessimistic about the national economy than men and that this difference remains after household income, occupational class, educational attainment and age are controlled for. Women in Britain are also more pessimistic about their own financial circumstances but this difference disappears once household income is controlled for. No differences have been found in the way men and women weigh economic variables when they vote.

## EVALUATIONS OF LEADERS

Leadership effects have long been a feature of analyses of voting behaviour in Britain. However, little attention has been paid to any potential gender differences. Media speculation about the reactions of men and women to leaders are commonplace but rarely subject to rigorous testing. This section uses evidence from focus groups, conducted prior to the 2005 British general election,[7] and the British Election Studies (BES) of 1997, 2001 and 2005 to assess whether we need gendered models of leadership evaluation.

Tony Blair has had a media image as a 'ladies' man' and it's widely assumed that the Labour Party's 1997 landslide election victory and re-election in 2001 owed a great deal to Tony Blair's personal popularity with women (*Telegraph* 30/09/2004; *Scotsman* 29/01/2005). During the 2005 election campaign there was unprecedented media interest in women voters.[8] A common story was that the 'relationship' between Tony Blair and women had broken down. A widely reported MORI poll commissioned by Fawcett found that 60 per cent of women were unhappy with Tony Blair. Women were also considered more likely to be affected by a lack of trust in Tony Blair, suggesting that they might value integrity above competence (Campbell and Lovenduski 2005). However, these polls did not compare women with men and cannot, therefore, accurately assess whether women were in fact more disaffected with Blair than men were. This section will compare men and women's responses to the party leaders to determine the accuracy of the differences reported in the media.

The analysis in this chapter is conducted using focus group data and BES data. The combination of qualitative and quantitative techniques allows an exploration of the potential gender differences in leader evaluation, because secondary data analysis alone might obscure any differences in language used by male and female respondents.[9] The focus group analysis is exploratory and cannot be used to make firm inferences about the British electorate.

### Focus group analysis

The candidate assessment component of the focus groups was designed to discover whether men and women would talk about political leaders in the same way. The candidate evaluation literature has developed a number of different schema that individuals might employ (Miller *et al.* 1996; Stokes 1966). The schema may be based on personal characteristics and appearances, on perceived competence or integrity or upon policy positions or ideological commitments. The focus group research attempted to establish whether the same schema could be applied to men and women.

During the ninety-minute sessions, respondents often mentioned leaders without prompting. In addition photographs of each of the three main party leaders were distributed and the participants were asked to brainstorm the words that came to mind and to write them down. There was a noticeable difference between the results of the general conversation and the brainstorming activity. In the main discussion, the comments about Tony Blair were generally negative and few comments were made about the other party leaders. However, in the brainstorming session respondents were often surprised that they had attributed positive characteristics to Tony Blair. There was little difference between the way men and women talked about party leaders. Men were more likely to complain that Tony

Blair was 'too right wing'. When asked what one issue they would like to raise with the party leaders one male respondent said:

I would ask Tony Blair, Do you remember Clause Four? Great idea that was. Any chance of reintroducing that?

Comments of this kind tended to come from older male respondents, there were five such comments from men respondents and none from women respondents; women's complaints about Tony Blair were more likely to focus on moral principles. Negative statements about Tony Blair were very common in all of the discussions. He was described variously as a 'yuppie barrister, liar, child-killer, smarmy and evangelical.' However, when asked to brainstorm their reactions to his picture respondents tended to identify more positive characteristics.

Statements such as these were typical:

I have got liar for Blair, weasel, no principles and running as fugitive interestingly. I have also got presidential and that is the only thing I have circled out of the three, because – I said this before – I think he is an incredibly clever man. Clever in the image he portrays, what he taps into his style, the fact that he doesn't say.

And Blair, out of the three – I mean I hate to say this because I agree with everything you've got to say about the war and everybody despises him – but there is something very presidential about him and statesman like. I think he plays that well.

And you had a surprise too? What was that? Yeah, because I've just got too many nice comments about Tony Blair!

Far fewer comments were made about Michael Howard and Charles Kennedy. Many of the responses to Michael Howard associated him with the past. One respondent said

Whereas with Michael Howard on the other hand, it seems like him out of a eighties movie or something

and

And Howard is... he is the minister of unemployment in the nasty party.

Again no particular differences between the sexes were evident. Responses to Charles Kennedy seemed to reflect recent media reporting. He was commonly referred to as drunk or dozy.

And Kennedy I just think is a guy to go to the pub with, have a couple of pints. I put drunk.

And I look at Kennedy appears sleepy too, you know?

This exploratory analysis of leadership evaluations does not suggest that women were more likely than men to have a personal or emotionally based evaluation schema than men. Men and women both used personal and issue-based criteria for evaluating candidates. Very little was said about the Conservative and Liberal Democrat party leaders. The comments about Charles Kennedy were much in line with the media framing of his character, particularly the references to his alcohol consumption. Overall, any differences between the way men and women described the leaders were minimal.

The qualitative research did not suggest any gender differences in leadership evaluation. The following section will test whether any gender differences in leadership evaluations are evident in the 1997 to 2005 British Election Studies.

### British Election Study analysis 1997–2005

Figure 6.1 shows the average response to the 'Tony Blair feelings thermometer' question between 1997 and 2005. Respondents were asked to place themselves on a scale on which zero represented a strong disliking and ten represented a strong liking of Tony Blair. The middle value – 5 – was removed from the analysis in case sex differences in neutral responses biased the results. The most evident pattern in Figure 6.1 is that Tony Blair's popularity fell consistently between 1997 and 2005. In each election there is a small gender difference, with women slightly less likely to respond positively to Tony Blair than men; the difference is virtually negligible in the 2005 sample. The differences between the sexes were tested for statistical significance. The difference between the sexes is only significant at the aggregate level in 1997.[10]

The analysis was repeated on separate samples of respondents by birth cohort. The difference between the sexes was only significant within the group of respondents born between 1906 and 1945. Women in the older group were more likely to have positive feelings about John Major and negative feelings about Tony Blair than men in the same group. The older women had an average of 5.58 on the 'feelings towards John Major' scale, compared with an average score of 4.68 for older men. The older women's average rating of Tony Blair was 6.26 compared to an average score of 7.06 for older men. The differences between older men and women were significant at the 0.001 level.[11]

In order to establish the underlying causes of the gender differences in feelings towards Tony Blair, a series of regressions were conducted and are presented in Table 6.5. The sex difference, where older women rated Tony Blair more negatively than the rest of the sample, persisted after each round of independent variables were included. The sex variable only became insignificant when a dummy variable for women born before 1946 was included. The independent variables measuring age when completed full-time education and whether the respondent had ever been in paid employment for more than ten hours a week did not remove the sex difference. Thus, older women were less keen on Tony Blair regardless of their education and employment history. Finally a battery of terms measuring political attitudes and allegiances were included and they did not remove the sex difference; thus older women's dislike of Tony Blair was not simply a function of their political beliefs. It would seem that the traditional gender gap was evident in leadership evaluations in 1997. Older generations of women rated Tony Blair less

Figure 6.1 Feelings about Tony Blair, by sex, 1997–2001

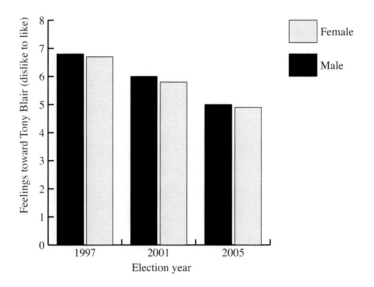

highly than other members of the electorate.

The aggregate level traditional gender gap in leadership evaluations was not statistically significant in the 2001 or 2005 BESs. The lack of a traditional gap might be the result of older women warming to Tony Blair or, more likely, the rest of the population cooling; alternatively, the lack of a gap might be the result of cohort replacement. The older generations of women who have more hostile attitudes to Tony Blair and are more likely to vote for the Conservative Party might have been replaced by younger women among whom the traditional gender gap is not evident. The reduced sample size of the older generations in the 2001 and 2005 BES might explain the lack of statistical significance. In order to test for cohort effects, the 2001 and 2005 BESs were combined and feelings towards Blair were compared by sex. Women born in the periods 1916–1925 and 1936–1945 were significantly less likely to rate Blair highly than men born at the same time.

Overall, the analysis of leadership evaluations undertaken in this chapter has demonstrated that men and women seem to apply the same criteria when judging candidates. The only significant differences in leadership evaluations were found amongst older respondents, where women were less likely to rate Tony Blair favourably than men. There was no evidence that younger women were more 'pro' Blair than younger men. The pattern that emerges is one of a traditional gender generation gap that is in decline.

In order to assess the impact of evaluations of leaders on vote choice, party political variables were added to the logistic regression presented in Table 6.6. Feelings towards the Labour Party had a just significant effect on the vote choice of men and not women in the 2001 BES. Attitudes toward European monetary union had a just

Table 6.5: Regression on feelings towards Tony Blair (1997 BES)[12]

| Independent variables | Model 1 | | Model 2 | | Model 3 | | Model 4 | | Model 5 | |
|---|---|---|---|---|---|---|---|---|---|---|
| | Beta | SE | Beta | SE | Beta | SE | Beta | SE | Beta | SE |
| Sex | -0.06** | 0.13 | -0.06** | 0.13 | -0.07** | 0.13 | -0.06** | 0.13 | -0.06** | 0.12 |
| Age | | | 0.05* | 0.004 | 0.007 | 0.004 | 0.002 | 0.004 | 0.05* | 0.004 |
| Education (age completed) | | | | | 0.11*** | 0.04 | 0.11*** | 0.04 | 0.06* | 0.04 |
| Never had a job for over 10hrs a week | | | | | | | -0.03 | 0.38 | -0.02 | 0.36 |
| Liberal attitudes | | | | | | | | | 0.08** | 0.02 |
| Socialist attitudes | | | | | | | | | 0.35*** | 0.10 |
| Feelings toward the Labour party | | | | | | | | | 0.12*** | 0.006 |
| n | 2054 | | 2054 | | 2031 | | 2031 | | 1964 | |
| R² | 0.006 | | 0.006 | | 0.02 | | 0.02 | | 0.17 | |

***Differences significant at the 0.001 level
** Differences significant at the 0.01 level
* Differences significant at the 0.05 level

significant effect on the vote choice on men and not women, as did self-placement on the left/right scale. Evaluations of government performance on education, health and pensions had a significant effect on the vote choice of women and not men: a step down the performance scale reduces the chance of a woman voting for the Labour Party by 80 per cent. Female respondents who stated that health or education was their most important election issue were five times more likely to vote for the Labour Party than respondents who didn't. In both groups, the model predicted vote choice over 95 per cent accurately and the Nagelkerke $R^2$ was 0.93 for both men and women; however, the sample size was extremely small, due in large part to the low turnout in the 2001 BES. The regression was repeated with the non-significant variables excluded to attempt to reduce the missing values.

The model correctly predicted 95 per cent or more of respondents' votes for the Conservative or Labour Party and the Nagelkerke $R^2$ was 0.92 for both men and women. The sample size was marginally improved, with 477 men and 455 women, but this was insufficient for further sub-division into respondents born before and after World War Two. Feelings toward the Labour Party had the same effect on the vote choice of men and women. For each step up the Labour Party evaluation scale, the respondent became three times more likely to vote for the Labour party. Feelings about the Conservative Party had the same impact on the vote choice of men and women. For each step up the Conservative Party evaluation scale the respondent becomes 50 per cent less likely to vote for the Labour Party. The combined response to government performance on the economy, inflation and taxation had a significant effect on the vote choice of women and not men, a difference not predicted by theory. Feelings about Tony Blair had a significant

Table 6.6: Logistic regression of vote (Conservative or Labour) and attitudes towards the parties and issue position in the 2001 general election, by sex[13]

| Sex | Independent variables | Exp(B) |
|---|---|---|
| Male | Feelings towards the Labour party | 2.619*** |
| | Feelings towards the Conservative party | .450*** |
| | Respondent feels there is a gap between what they expect and what they get | 1.136 |
| | Feelings towards Tony Blair | 1.950* |
| | Feelings towards William Hague | .666 |
| | Economic expectations self next year | .980 |
| | Economic expectations country next year | 2.152 |
| | Attitude towards European monetary union | .199* |
| | Attitude towards membership of the EU | 1.385 |
| | Self placement left/right scale | .630* |
| | Labour on the left/right scale | 1.160 |
| | Labour on the tax/spend scale | .862 |
| | Government performance on education health and pensions | 1.172 |
| | Government performance on economic issues | .311* |
| | NHS or Education most important election issue | .347 |
| | Constant | 1.302 |
| Female | Feelings towards the Labour party | 3.334*** |
| | Feelings towards the Conservative party | .486*** |
| | Respondent feels there is a gap between what they expect and what they get | 1.102 |
| | Feelings towards Tony Blair | 1.151 |
| | Feelings towards William Hague | .917 |
| | Economic expectations self next year | 2.353 |
| | Economic expectations country next year | .467 |
| | Attitude towards European monetary union | 1.097 |
| | Attitude towards membership of the EU | .987 |
| | Self placement left/right scale | .565 |
| | Labour on the left/right scale | 1.589 |
| | Labour on the tax/spend scale | .985 |
| | Government performance on education health and pensions | .185** |
| | Government performance on economic issues | 5.146** |
| | NHS or Education most important election issue | 10.540** |
| | Constant | .012 |

effect upon the vote choice of men and not women. Sample size issues prohibit further sub-group analysis. Future research should attempt to establish whether leadership evaluations do in fact have a stronger impact upon the vote choices of men than women.

Table 6.6i: Logistic regression of vote (Conservative or Labour) and attitudes towards the parties and issue position in the 2001 general election, by sex (insignificant parameters excluded)

| Sex | Independent variables | Exp(B) |
|---|---|---|
| Male | Feelings towards the Labour party | 2.798*** |
| | Feelings towards the Conservative party | .421*** |
| | Feelings towards Tony Blair | 1.727** |
| | Attitude towards European monetary union | .355** |
| | Self placement on the left/right scale | .570** |
| | Government performance health, education and pensions | .787 |
| | Government performance economy, inflation and taxation | .434 |
| | NHS or education most important election issue | .666 |
| | Constant | 3.349 |
| Female | Feelings towards the Labour party | 2.933*** |
| | Feelings towards the Conservative party | .445*** |
| | Feelings towards Tony Blair | 1.280 |
| | Attitude towards European monetary union | .839 |
| | Self placement on the left/right scale | .761 |
| | Government performance health, education and pensions | .357* |
| | Government performance economy, inflation and taxation | 3.547** |
| | NHS or education most important election issue | 4.331* |
| | Constant | .155 |

## SUMMARY

This chapter has established that women were more pessimistic about the national economy than men. The difference remains once socio-economic status is controlled for and is consistent with US findings. Women were more pessimistic about their own personal financial circumstances than men. That difference disappeared when household income was controlled for, indicating that the gap is attributable to women's lower incomes. Feelings about the national economy affected the vote choice of both men and women whereas personal financial circumstances did not impact upon the voting behaviour of either sex. Men and women appeared to employ the same schema when evaluating leaders. Women, particularly older women, rated Tony Blair less highly than men in the 1997, 2001 and 2005 elections but the gap was only statistically significant in 1997. There was weak evidence that men paid more attention to leadership evaluations when deciding how to vote than women. Future research should test this further using larger sample surveys.

## NOTES

1 The 2001 BES is analysed because it includes a range of questions about feelings towards the economy that don't have a middle/stayed the same/neither value. According to some research, women are more likely than men to choose the middle or don't know option and this can bias results (Mondak and Anderson 2004).

2 Respondents were asked to evaluate their own personal financial circumstances over the previous year.

3 Respondents were asked to evaluate the national economy over the past year.

4 Respondents were asked to evaluate what the expect from their own personal financial circumstances over the next year.

5 Respondents were asked to evaluate what the expect to happen to the national economy in the next year.

6 The independent variables in Table 6.4 are: sex (0=men 1=women), household income (1<£5000 to 12>£60000), Occupational class is measured using the respondent's Goldthorpe-Heath class schema compressed. Education is measured using age when completed full-time education.

7 Project funded by the British Academy, grant number 40355.

8 The 2005 election is discussed in more detail in the following chapter.

9 In total, six focus groups were conducted in the week of the 2005 British general election. There were two single-sex groups of mixed ages and four single-sex groups divided by aged under or over 45. The respondents were selected using stratified sampling from a recruitment form that included occupation and income. It is unlikely that the groups are representative of the British electorate as a whole but there was a mix of ethnicities, incomes and educational backgrounds. The background characteristics of the men and women were not systematically different and comparisons between men and women should not be problematic. The focus groups are described in more detail in the following chapter.

10 The sexes' feelings about the other main party leaders were also compared; any differences were small and not statistically significant.

11 The analysis was also conducted on ten-year cohorts. Women gave Blair lower ratings than men in all of the groups between 1906 and 1955. In the cohorts from 1955 to 1985, women gave Blair slightly higher ratings than men but the differences were not statistically significant.

12 There is evidence of multicollinearity in the models.

13 None of the bivariate correlations are above 0.6, indicating that multicollinearity is not a problem in the model.

# chapter seven | the 2005 british general election
## with kristi winters

The 2005 general election is analysed separately here for a number of reasons. First, validated turnout figures from the British Election Study (BES) were not available at the time of writing; therefore, all analysis is conducted on self-reported vote. Second, there was an unusual level of media attention focused upon women in the 2005 campaign (Campbell and Lovenduski October 2005). Finally, in addition to the analysis of quantitative data from the BES, a qualitative focus group project was undertaken in the run up to the 2005 election, the results of which are drawn upon here. The qualitative research complements the quantitative analysis by providing insight into the motivations and explanations for vote choices as voters themselves conceive them. The qualitative approach is also helpful for refining our theories of gender and political behaviour.

It may be that men and women use different language to describe politics or they may tend to raise different issues. Thus, this chapter is an analysis of the 2005 election from several perspectives, testing the theories and hypotheses outlined in the preceding chapters.

The first section of this chapter uses the data that is thus far available, to test whether there is evidence of a gender gap or a gender generation gap in the 2005 election. The second section is an analysis of focus group data, examining whether men and women thought about and/or talked about the election and politics generally in different ways.

## A GENDER GAP IN 2005?

In the run up to the 2005 general election, the parties and the media were unusually interested in women voters. Attempts to target or 'woo' women's votes were highlighted by the media coverage and became a central feature of the campaign. 'Worcester woman' returned, accompanied by 'letdown woman' and 'do-it-all woman'. These catch phrases allowed the framing of women as a target group of voters. But there was no 'Mondeo man', and men as a group were generally absent from the parties' campaigns and from the newspaper reporting (*Observer*, 20.2.05; *Telegraph*, 30.3.05; *Independent*, 01.4.05; *Mirror*, 15.4.05). Thus, women became a key target group in the press. ICM polls put women's support for Labour just 1 point above men's. Women were frequently described as feeling let down by Labour and let down by Tony Blair in particular. There were conflicting reports of women's voting intentions in the media. Overall the vacillation in women's voting intentions reported in the media was probably a result of poor research methods. Women's 'disillusionment' was most often described without any comparison to men (*Daily Mail*, 28.2.05; *News of the World*, 13.3.05). Reports of poll evidence that women were unhappy with Tony Blair frequently did not offer comparable data on men. This sloppy reporting created the impression that women, as a group, were more likely to switch away from Labour. The aggregate MORI data, made available after the election, indicate that no such switch took place. Indeed, according to this data the opposite occurred. In fact Norris's gender generation gap is evident in the MORI data and for the first time it appears that there was an aggregate level gender gap of six points.[1] The pooled MORI campaign opinion polls, presented in Tables 7.1 and 7.2, provide an exceptionally large sample size suitable for subgroup analysis. In the months preceding the election, MORI data suggested that, for the first time in the postwar period, a balance of more women than men were likely to vote Labour. Table 7.1 outlines the voting patterns found by MORI among men and women of different ages. Within each age group, a gender gap figure is produced and displayed in the final column; a positive figure indicates that women in that group were more likely to support Labour then men. Tables 7.1 and 7.2 indicate that the traditional gender gap in Britain has indeed reversed and that, overall, women are now more likely to vote for the Labour Party than men. Table 7.1 shows that women under the age of fifty four were more likely than men to vote for the Labour Party, a trend that is even stronger in the younger age groups. Older women were more likely than men to say that they were going to vote for the Conservative Party. This trend confirms the pattern that was already evident in 1997 and 2001. Table 7.2 demonstrates that 2005 is the first election in which the gender generation gap meant that more women than men voted Labour. Could this gradual change in the gender gap be attributable to a successful effort to target women voters mounted by the Labour Party? Certainly since 1997 the Labour Party has campaigned on issues that are known to be higher priorities for women voters than for men. Women are more likely than men to say that health and education are the most important election issues, although these issues remain important to both men and women (Campbell 2004). If the MORI predictions are validated, then it may be that British elections are moving towards the American model, where a gender gap has been evident at the aggregate level since 1980.

The MORI data in Tables 7.1 and 7.2 clearly support the gender generation gap thesis. The British election study has a rolling pre-election study that does not provide validated vote figures but offers an additional data point. The BES rolling data in presented in Table 7.3. There is a statistically significant aggregate level gender gap in the BES rolling data of 7 percentage points; this is very close to the MORI figure, which was 6 percentage points.

Table 7.1: Voting preference by sex and age, 2005

| Age | Sex | Conservative | Labour | Liberal Democrat | Con/Lab Gender Gap |
|-----|-----|--------------|--------|------------------|--------------------|
| 18–24 | Men | 33 | 34 | 25 | 20 |
| | Women | 22 | 43 | 26 | |
| 25–34 | Men | 29 | 33 | 27 | 18 |
| | Women | 21 | 43 | 28 | |
| 35–54 | Men | 31 | 36 | 22 | 8 |
| | Women | 27 | 40 | 25 | |
| 55+ | Men | 40 | 33 | 20 | 0 |
| | Women | 41 | 34 | 20 | |
| All | Men | 34 | 34 | 23 | 6 |
| | Women | 32 | 38 | 22 | |

The gender gap is calculated as Conservative lead over Labour among men minus Conservative lead over Labour among women (per cent Con men - per cent Lab men) minus (per cent Con women - per cent Lab women).

Source: MORI Final aggregate analysis from the pooled campaign surveys 16th May 2005 Total n=17,595. www.mori.com

Table 7.2: The Con-Lab gender gap 1992–2005

| Year | Size of the gender gap |
|------|------------------------|
| 1992 | -5.8 |
| 1997 | -4.5 |
| 2001 | -1.1 |
| 2005 | +6.0 |

The figures for 1992–2001 are calculated using the series of British Election Studies, validated voters only. The figure for 2005 is estimated using the MORI Final aggregate analysis from the pooled campaign surveys 16th May 2005 Total n. 17,595. www.mori.com

Table 7.3: Party of vote by sex (BES pre-campaign rolling data 2005)

| Sex | Party of vote | | | Total |
|-----|--------|--------------|---------|-------|
| | Labour | Conservative | Lib Dem | |
| Men | 38.3% | 36.2% | 25.5% | 100% |
| Women | 40.7% | 31.4% | 27.9% | 100% |
| All | 39.5% | 33.7% | 26.8% | 100% |

n=4493
Differences significant at the 0.01 level chi-square test

Table 7.4: Party of vote by sex and age-group (BES pre-campaign rolling data 2005)

| Age | Sex | Party of vote | | | Total |
|-----|-----|---------|--------------|---------|-------|
| | | Labour | Conservative | Lib Dem | |
| 18–24* | Men | 37.5% | 34.4% | 28.1% | 100% |
| | Women | 43.7% | 22.6% | 33.7% | 100% |
| 25–34*** | Men | 37.5% | 36% | 26.5% | 100% |
| | Women | 41.3% | 20.6% | 38.1% | 100% |
| 35–44 | Men | 41.4% | 34% | 24.5% | 100% |
| | Women | 44.4% | 26.8% | 28.9% | 100% |
| 45–54 | Men | 40.5% | 32.3% | 27.3% | 100% |
| | Women | 37.4% | 34.9% | 27.7% | 100% |
| 55–59 | Men | 38.2% | 35.9% | 25.8% | 100% |
| | Women | 41.0% | 33.6% | 25.4% | 100% |
| 60–64 | Men | 35.3% | 41.7% | 23.1% | 100% |
| | Women | 42.5% | 39.8% | 17.7% | 100% |
| 65+ | Men | 35.6% | 41.3% | 23.1% | 100% |
| | Women | 33.0% | 43.4% | 22.2% | 100% |

n=4493
*** Differences significant at the 0.001 level chi-square test
** Differences significant at the 0.01 level chi-square test
* Differences significant at the 0.05 level chi-square test

In Table 7.4 there is a statistically significant gender generation gap in the under-thirty-fives. The traditional gender gap, where more women than men voted Conservative, is evident in the over sixty-fives but it is not statistically significant.

There is an 18-point gender gap among the eighteen to twenty-five year old respondents and a 19-point gap among the twenty-five to thirty-four year old respondents. Tables 7.1 to 7.4 have provided evidence of both an aggregate level gender gap and a gender generation gap in the 2005 general election. The data sources used both had large sample sizes and were collected using random sampling techniques. It would appear therefore that the 2005 election may have been a turning point for the gender generation gap, which had previously only been evident within age-groups and not at an aggregate level. It may be that the 2005 election is part of a global trend identified by Inglehart and Norris whereby women in industrial nations are moving to the left of men (Inglehart and Norris 2000). However, we should be aware that the gender differences in party of vote are likely to be affected by electoral context such as issue salience. The underlying causes of the 2005 gender gap will be explored in the following two sections of this chapter.

Table 7.5: Multinomial logistic regression of party of vote in 2005 (BES 2005 rolling-pre-election)

| Independent variables | Model 1 | | Model 2 | | Model 3 | | Model 4 | |
|---|---|---|---|---|---|---|---|---|
| | Con/Lab Exp B | Lib/Lab Exp B | Con/Lab Exp B | Lib/Lab Exp B | Con/Lab Exp B | Lib/Lab Exp B | Con/Lab Exp B | Lib/Lab Exp B |
| Sex | 1.2** | 0.97 | 1.23** | 0.96 | 1.18* | 0.93 | 1.06 | 0.90 |
| Age | | | 0.99*** | 1.01** | 0.98*** | 0.99* | 0.98*** | 0.99 |
| Age finished education | | | | | 1.16*** | 1.28*** | 1.08** | 1.30*** |
| Household income | | | | | | | 1.11*** | 0.99 |
| Cox and Snell Pseudo R² | 0.005 | 0.005 | 0.015 | 0.015 | 0.032 | 0.032 | 0.053 | 0.053 |
| n | 4504 | 4504 | 4504 | 4504 | 4249 | 4249 | 3823 | 3823 |

***Significant at the 0.001 level
**Significant at the 0.01 level
*Significant at the 0.05 level

## THE CAUSES OF THE GENDER GAP

A gender gap is evident in the pre-election rolling BES data and the pre-election MORI data. Table 7.5 attempts to establish the underlying causes of the gap. The models presented in Table 7.5 contain only background characteristics and are not complete models of vote choice; this is reflected in the low pseudo-$R^2$ figures. There is not a statistically significant gender gap between Labour and Liberal Democrat vote in any of the models. Women were more likely to vote for the Labour party than the Conservative Party in models one to three. However, the gender gap is no longer significant when household income is controlled for, mirroring the findings presented in Chapter five. In the lowest income groups, men were more likely than women to vote for the Labour Party and women were more likely than men to vote for the Conservative Party, but the gap was not statistically significant. There was a statistically significant gender gap in the top income groups, where women were 5 per cent less likely than men to vote for the Conservative Party and 7 per cent more likely than men to vote for the Liberal Democrats. The results demonstrate that the three-party system operating in Britain is likely to prevent a large Conservative/Labour gender gap developing to match the gap in the United States. It would seem that there are significant differences that should be explored but the pattern and nature of that difference changes according to electoral context. The following section will establish whether there is evidence of gender differences in political attitudes using qualitative analysis.

## FOCUS GROUP RESEARCH

The analysis of focus group data finds that an 'ethics of care' approach based upon the theories of Carol Gilligan is still a useful mechanism for distinguishing between the ethics of men and women. Gilligan's *In a Different Voice* was written twenty-three years before this chapter. In that time the changes in the occupational and educational status of women that were already underway have accelerated to the point where women now constitute 46 per cent of the labour market and 54 per cent of university students (EOC 2005). However, there are still areas of inequality. The unequal distribution of women's unpaid caring work is well documented (EOC 2005: 14). In fact four out of five women undertake 79 per cent of housework in Britain (Diagnostics and Social Market Research Co-op 1999) and 66 per cent of childcare (O'Brien and Shemilt 2003). The research presented in this section indicates that the different socialisation processes experienced by men and women – or girls and boys – as a result of the sexual division of labour, continue to operate upon the psyches of the sexes and that the different lived experiences of men and women impact upon their political preferences. In our focus groups women were much more likely than men to raise the particular needs and experience of others when talking about politics. Men were more likely than women to talk about politics in an abstract/conceptual manner and to focus upon the economic dimensions of political decision-making. It would appear that although men and women's lives are now more alike than ever before, the psychological differences generated by women's disproportionate role in unpaid caring work, described by Gilligan, have remained intact.

As outlined in the introductory chapters of this book, feminist theorists provide models that illustrate the different experiences of women and men. Researchers studying the gender gap in the United States very often compare an 'ethics of care' approach developed from feminist theory to a rational-choice approach, where any gender differences in attitudes and behaviour can be accounted for by the different material interests of men and women. The analysis in this section will attempt to compare the two approaches.

Qualitative research techniques are employed here to establish whether there is any evidence that women and men think about politics in different ways. Do women tend to think about their personal connections more than men do when making political decisions? Do men tend to discuss politics using an abstract and disconnected framework?

The focus group research undertaken here attempts to assess whether there are any differences in political thinking between the sexes. However, focus groups yield conversational data and not thought processes. It is possible, and indeed likely, that participants will influence each other. Therefore, extrapolation from the group to the population is limited and this research is exploratory in nature.

### Methods

In the week preceding the 2005 general election six focus groups were conducted.[2]

The groups took place in London and Colchester, Essex. The groups were divided by sex and age. There were three groups of men and three groups of women. The groups were then sub-divided, with two groups of respondents under forty, two groups of respondents over forty and two mixed-age groups. The age dimension was included because testing Pippa Norris's gender-generation gap is an important element of this study and mixed-age groups might have obscured age differences. The participants were recruited by email and by paper flyer. All potential participants were asked to complete a brief questionnaire about their personal details. Stratified sampling techniques were then used to obtain a mix of educational, occupation and ethnic backgrounds. Participants were paid a nominal fee in the hope that this would encourage the participation of individuals from a broader range of backgrounds. The sampling did not yield a representative sample of the British public but broadly similar groups of men and women were generated, permitting comparisons by sex. In order to conduct a fair test of gender differences in responses, the same questions were asked in each of the groups according to a pre-designed interview schedule.

**Analysis**
Analysis of the focus group transcripts provides insight into the similarities and differences between the way men and women talk about politics. Beginning with the areas of commonality, all six groups stressed their disillusionment with formal politics. In every group political parties and politicians were criticised for being disingenuous. A theme resounded within the groups: dissatisfaction that the policies of the two major parties, Labour and the Conservatives, were virtually indistinguishable, and the desire for more ideological or principled politics. It was more common for men to lament the decline in ideology and for women to describe politicians as unprincipled.

Participants were sceptical about the campaign and its message. The campaign was described by one participant as a 'media bandwagon' and there was a general distaste for the commercialisation of politics:
> 'Politics is more or less commercialising, that is where the Sainsbury's manager comes in, because he's selling a product. Labour is a product and Conservative is a product. And "We have more chocolate than you." "No no. We put more cocoa in our chocolate."'[3]

A sense of alienation from politics was evident in all the transcripts.

When discussing politics more generally, men tended to focus upon traditional left–right issues. In the men under-forty group there was a long debate about taxation versus spending. The left-leaning members of the group advocated principles of fairness and justice based upon redistribution and a move to the left on the part of the Labour Party:
> 'Tax ought to be, if you look at it in tax terms, and not only is it an excellent wealth generation terms it should be an excellent electoral weapon.... It should

be something you stand up and say, we will do this, we will tax you fifty per cent because you're earning that much and you can afford it. Fifty per cent is fair, that's fine…What are they paying them for? You are paying these taxes so you can have good public services so don't have to go down the public–private road for hospitals. It means we can have a decent rail network, etc. etc… For me the Labour Party is there to promote social justice, is to challenge inequalities in society, to make the income more redistribution of wealth, is to challenge pressures that people faced daily.'

The right-leaning members talked about how best to use tax funds and the appropriate role of government in terms of providing services:

'I don't want more taxes and I'm going to vote Labour now if I can but that's not because... all the money I earned anyway it is not sufficient and if tax is going to take away a lot of it then it's not justice to me in any case. The way in which money has to be generated are different, and how that money is spent is also very critical. Public spending doesn't guarantee that we will get it all, that we will get buses and schools and things like that. In fact, it's often more basic than that... No I think that taxes should in fact be reduced and there should be more efficiency, but the state does not just provide everything because it is often not efficient enough to provide everything.'

There was a demand for the parties to address these issues more directly. There was very little mention of men's own personal circumstances, family members or mention of others to whom they were connected. Younger men touch upon how they thought having a 'family' would affect their political views in the abstract. There was a sense that taxation and valuing lower taxes would be associated with being a parent. Discussing taxation one young male participant said:

'but I don't think it affects me at all. I'm not a family person so nothing they do will really affect me, the increase in taxation I won't notice really. But it does fascinate me.'

Another participant said, 'I think that's true but if I had a family, I think the financial side of it would matter.' The stress on personal finances, taxation and family life was not raised in the women's groups.

When discussing politics generally women tended not to define politics as simply party political, but instead put an emphasis upon personal and family relationships. The role of relationships in terms of perceptions of politics was evident from the start of the women's focus groups. The first question asked in all the groups was: 'Please introduce yourself and say something about how you first became aware of politics.'

Men were most likely to speak of their initial political awareness in terms of reference to themselves. For example,

'I have been interested in politics ever since I can remember…' or

'I can't really remember when I first became interested in politics, but it was certainly from the age of ten onwards. I was aware of political parties and different sorts of opinions, and my views have matured since then.'

Alternatively men cited a political event, such as a general election or the miners' strikes as their earliest impetus to political awareness. Women, on the other hand, were far more likely to cite a familial relationship:

'I was brought up in a Labour background. Dad was Trade Union through and through, but that all fell through in the early 80s. He packed it all in, said "No good. No good," and even our political views started to change then,'

'I suppose I became really aware when my parents – or my mother, actually – was on the local Labour Party's campaign and I got roped in as a seven-year-old posting leaflets through doors, helping her campaign.'

Like men, women also cited political events such as the miners' strike or elections as the impetus to their political awareness.

Unique to the women's groups were descriptions, sometimes in detail, of their interactions with others as well as how friends and family influence their political opinions:

'I mean we might not talk about party politics and we might not talk about politicians, but political issues, my daughter and I – not row about, but hiss and spit and curse all the time. It isn't always talked about as politics. It might be talked about as issues.'

'I do listen to other people. I listen to my partner and I tend to go with his views. Really sad, because I don't have that actual active interest in politics.'

'I have voted Green once and I discuss with my partner so we don't cancel each other out in terms of votes.'

'Well, I'm quite lazy as well, but I'm really busy – but I'm lucky because lots of friends and family members are very politically active and involved, and I feel sort of intelligent in their approach and their attitudes to politics. And so I just ask them a lot because they are not all things that I get to understand and ask questions and sort of feel that I can.'

The older women talked about the parties moving closer together, ideologically, in the same way as men did but they were talking about the disengagement of their children and not themselves or 'others'.

'I have two adult children, and one of the things that really concerned me from their mid-teens onwards, was their total lack of engagement with politics.'

Self-interest is less narrowly defined by the women's groups, such as 'I want to pay less tax' and more about direct experience of government services. In the example below the respondent is talking about what got her daughter interested in politics.

'When it starts to affect you personally. This is when you start to get quite alarmed really, some of the things that are going on. And I think this is it. Until it actually affects you personally…with the young ones, you know, they wouldn't think about it.'

The older women participants discussed disillusionment with politicians and parties in much the same language as men but the tended to replace themselves in the discussion with their children. (The 'they' in this section are their collective children.)

'But we've talked about this and they say that their main reason for not engaging in politics is because they feel that they cannot make a difference; that politicians aren't principled. That politicians no longer stand for principles, so you can't choose this party because their principles map onto yours. It's all about degrees of difference and I take their point. If you look at politician-speak, it just seems to me that 95 per cent of the time they are talking to try and get your vote. They are not talking about the principles behind what they are deciding to do, or the issues. They are saying what they think you want to hear so that you will vote for them.'

The women's groups tended to raise political issues in relation to others they had personal relationships with. Thus the first issue raised by the older women was housing for first-time buyers and how their children would struggle to buy. Anti-social behaviour and discipline in schools were brought up but discussed in relation to their own children. When asked if anything was missing from a list of the most important issues a respondent raised childcare and her own daughter.

'The issues for me are chiefly childcare. I mean I work through a time when my daughter's in a nursery and it's like paying a second mortgage.'

All of the groups raised environmental issues but only the women's groups stressed their children or grandchildren's futures.

'This is the sort of thing that really alarms me. We're heading for sort of... perhaps not in my generation but I've got grandchildren. And I think about them.'

Motherhood and parenthood were stressed continually in the women's groups. There was only one mention of a parental relationship in the men's groups.

'I mean you always think – you know being a mother or something – you always think, 'I'd do it differently than you.'

Again children and motherhood are central to the discussion. Public services were discussed in terms of personal experience and family relationships.

'now having a son, anything to do with education, and also health care. Having an absolutely wonderful hospital but being thanked by the nurses for not having to ask them how to manage my son because I have experience from doing it. And seeing the stress that everyone is under, the nurses, things like that.'

Men's conversations were not completely devoid of familial relationships, however they were used as an illustrative rather than explanatory factor. One of the fathers in the mixed group cited his inability to get an appointment with the NHS as an example of its inefficiency:

'But otherwise look at the NHS. It's a black hole and it has been two months since I've been trying to get a simple appointment with a doctor for my daughter's wart on her foot and it's not available. And I am going to have to pay £100 tomorrow and this is for a kid.'

The other familial relationship mentioned was in the group of older men to support the idea that it is a civic duty to vote:

'No. Everybody should vote. Even if you feel it's a poor choice, it's still *the* choice you get every couple of years, you know? Local election, parliamentary election. People (expletive) died for this, to get us this far. Especially my wife always says, "I vote because I feel I have to. People died for wanting to get the vote."'

Overall, the most profound differences between women and men weren't necessarily matters of content but instead of motivation. Men and women both raised taxation, education, health, the economy and the environment. Women were slightly more likely than men to discuss health and education and men were slightly more likely than women to raise taxation, Europe and the economy. However, there was a striking difference in the *way* men and women discussed these issues. Women made continual references to personal relationships whereas such connections were virtually absent from the men's discussions.

In particular there were a couple of key conversations that help illustrate the pivotal role of parenthood upon gender differences in attitudes to politics. A number of women emphasised how motherhood had altered their perceptions and interests and a small number of young men suggested that having a family might alter their political perspective. The analysis in the previous chapter demonstrated that middle-income mothers were more likely to vote for the Labour Party in 2001 than middle-income fathers and that this accounted for a significant portion of the gender generation gap. The results of focus group analysis suggest that traditional sex roles, where women undertake most of the caring work for young children (and for other dependent people) and men take more responsibility for financial provision still has a powerful impact upon political behaviour. The discussions suggest that women and men weigh up different considerations when deciding how to vote and that, depending upon party platforms and issue salience, these could translate into gender differences in vote choice.

However, a cautionary note should be included. There were considerable differences in the focus and nature of the conversations had by groups of men and women but we cannot ascertain the impact of the group interaction. Towards the end of the discussion when asked if anything had been missed off a list of important issues a younger man said

'I would like to see health, more than now. I know I didn't say that before but if I had thought about it properly, I think that would have been one of my issues I think.'

The younger men's discussion did not dwell on health issues and it may be that there was a group effect where men were less willing to discuss certain issues, such as health and perhaps children's issues, with each other. Further individual survey analysis could help to establish whether this is the case by probing the differences evident within the focus group data.

## SUMMARY

A survey of the focus group transcripts and the summary above indicates that the choice between rational-choice versus 'ethics of care' account of men's and women's political attitudes and behaviour is simplistic. Both men and women attempted to discuss politics in terms of morality or right and wrong. Women tended to approach the subject by contextualising, using examples of people they knew, whereas men tended to remove themselves and try to think abstractly. Men were not necessarily more self-interested but they were more likely to remove themselves and other concrete individuals from the discussion. Women were more likely to try to use examples from their own experience and relationships. Professional middle-class men espoused left-leaning political values that might not have represented their own self-interest but they tended not to attempt to think about how particular politics would impact upon particular groups or individuals. This difference is likely to have its basis in the sexual division of labour. The differences tended not to be apparent when leaders were evaluated. Both men and women combined issue and personal issues when evaluating leaders. The real difference was when issues and policies were discussed. The focus group research demonstrates that men and women tend to think about politics in different ways. How these differences translate into vote choice is not immediately apparent. The results do suggest however, that the Labour Party's focus on health and education and the reduced emphasis on traditional ideologies might have made the party particularly attractive to women. Women still vote for the Conservative Party in roughly equal numbers to men, but this research shows that they may have different reasons or explanations for doing so. It is possible that an individualistic right-leaning ideology is not a good explanation of women's right-leaning preferences. Women tend to emphasise relationships and family connections and right-wing women might believe that keeping state intervention to a minimum best protects families. Future survey research should explore these issues further by asking men and women to select policy preferences on the basis of whether they best serve the interests of themselves, their family, individuals in society generally, society generally or specified groups such as children, mothers or first-time buyers. Such an approach may help us to unpick whether the differences apparent in the qualitative research undertaken here is reflected in the population.

## CONCLUSION

This chapter has demonstrated that there was a gender gap in attitudes and voting intentions prior to the 2005 British general election. The gap can be partially accounted for by middle and high income women failing to support the Conservative party in equal numbers to middle and high income men. There is not a measure of parenthood in the 2005 pre-election rolling study so it is not possible to establish whether this was the motherhood effect, evident in the 2001 BSA.

The exploratory focus group analysis illustrated that men and women tend to talk about politics and political issues in different ways. Women tend to employ a connected, contextual framework for thinking about politics, whereas men tend to talk in abstract, disconnected terms. Future research should develop quantitative measures to test these differences further.

## NOTES

1   MORI and BES figures are used in this chapter but any findings will need to be checked against the validated BES turnout figures, which were not available at the time of writing.
2   Project funded by the British Academy, grant number 40355.
3   All quotes are reported verbatim.

# conclusions

There are three broad areas to consider when drawing conclusions about the relationship between gender and vote in Britain. First, is there a relationship between gender and vote and if so what are its causes? Second, what contribution does this research make to the study of women and politics? Finally, what do these findings tell us about the study of voting behaviour more generally?

## THE RELATIONSHIP BETWEEN GENDER AND VOTE

The overall research question that this book has sought to answer is 'in what way and to what extent are women's political preferences different to men's as expressed in voting behaviour?'. The conclusion can be drawn that men and women's political preferences and voting behaviour do differ, but the relationship is complex and is evident within sub-groups rather than at the aggregate level. Overall evidence was found of a traditional gender gap in decline: older women were found to be more conservative than older men. Evidence was also found of the emergence of a modern gender gap, where younger women were more left-leaning than younger men, in attitudes and sometimes vote choice.

Gender differences were found in issue priorities. As predicted by feminist theory and feminist empirical research, women were more likely than men to prioritise issues such as health and education and men were more likely to emphasise the economy. Furthermore, younger women appear to be more left-leaning in their political attitudes and feminist orientations than younger men. The gender gap in attitudes is partially matched by a gender gap in voting behaviour. Among individuals born after 1946, women were more likely to support the Labour Party than men; among those born before 1946, however, women were more likely to support the Conservative Party than men. However, this gap was not consistent across all age-groups and elections. In 2001, the gender generation gap was not evident amongst the eighteen to twenty-four year-old respondents but it was among those aged twenty-five to forty-four. The lack of a contemporary gender gap in the under-twenty-fives may be partially accounted for by the fact that middle-income mothers[1] were more likely to support the Labour Party than middle-income fathers, and middle-income mothers are likely to be over twenty-five.[2] Thus, there is little evidence of an aggregate-level gender gap, whereby being a women significantly increases the chances that an individual would vote for one party or another; but instead we see a complex pattern of sub-group effects, where sex interacts with other background characteristics to produce gendered political behaviours and attitudes.

Analysis of the results of quantitative secondary data analysis outlined above provides a description of patterns of gendered attitudes and choices but it does not provide a comprehensive account of their underlying causes. Thus, the focus group project allowed us to identify factors that were not measured in the surveys but were perhaps driving the differences apparent in the quantitative data. The results of the focus groups were enlightening. We had not expected the differences between the way men and women talk about politics to be so profound and pervasive. No real differences were apparent in the way men and women talked about party leaders, they were discussed using both personal and issue-based criteria. But real gender differences were evident when issues and policies were discussed.

When talking about politics, it seemed that men tended to employ the liberal conception of the rational autonomous individual as the subject of political action. Irrespective of whether they had a socialist or laissez-faire position, men tended to abstract from the specific needs and interests of particular groups in society. Women, on the other hand, tended to conceptualise politics in terms of its effects upon a web of relationships. They were more likely to highlight the needs of dependent and vulnerable individuals, be they children or others. Women tended to evaluate policy performance through the interests and experience of people they knew or cared for.

It seems plausible that these underlying differences might explain both the traditional gender gap and the modern gender gap in attitudes. The results of this research indicate that gender is a factor that shapes political behaviour but the nature and direction of any difference is dependent upon the social and political environment of the time. Older and younger women in the focus groups appeared to think about politics in terms of how political decisions might sustain or even fracture a connected web of relationships. When women's involvement in the public sphere was severely restricted, they may have been more likely to support a style of politics that they felt protected their families from outside interference. In the modern context, where many more women are in employment, education and increasingly in political life, women may have begun to see politics as something that can help to sustain and support relationships, through better-quality childcare, health services or education.

Perhaps men are less concerned with the interests of specific groups because the responsibility for caring work still overwhelming falls to women and is assigned to the private sphere, and thus is not a proper area for political consideration. From this perspective, citizens are not conceptualised as embodied, gendered or dependent. This style of politics is about pursuing what is right for all in an abstract uniform sense and is juxtaposed against a feminised politics that recognises and is concerned with group difference. As long as the sexual division of labour persists, it is likely that gender differences in political attitudes and behaviour will remain, due to the far-reaching impact of childhood socialisation upon the psyches of the sexes.

However, the sexual division of labour is not the only persistent difference in the life experience of the sexes. Women tend to be found in different occupations from men, with more women employed in the public sector. Evidence presented in Chapter five demonstrated that women's public sector employment had a stronger impact upon their vote choice than men's. Thus, it is possible that the sexual division of paid labour plays as important a role as the sexual division of unpaid caring work in forming gendered political attitudes. It is not possible using currently available datasets to establish whether differences in socialisation, patterns of parenthood or employment account for the differences we saw in the conceptualisation of politics. Furthermore, the results of the focus group research require further exploration, because it is possible that the differences could be attributed to group interaction effects. Thus, there is a real need to design survey or experimental research that tests these findings further. Future research should establish whether men and women use different conceptual frameworks when thinking about politics and whether socialisation, parenthood, occupation or a combination of all three provide the best account of the complex gender differences in attitudes and vote choice outlined in this book.

The combination of the quantitative secondary data analysis and the focus group research suggests that the political parties and the media are right to identify target subgroups of men and women at election time. However, the media's emphasis on women's evaluations of Tony Blair in 2005, discussed in Chapter six, was misplaced. There was little difference in the leader evaluations of men and women and only the oldest cohorts of women gave Tony Blair more negative ratings than men, reflecting a traditional gender gap in decline. The media's focus upon attempts to 'woo' women voters did not take full account of the differences between women. The differences in political preferences between the sexes were most apparent within sub-groups and not at an aggregate level. Younger women were more likely than the rest of the electorate to prioritise education, whilst older women were most likely to prioritise health. Men in general placed more emphasis on the economy and the European Union than women. Younger women, women working in the public sector and middle-income mothers were all more likely to vote for the Labour Party than the Conservative Party. Thus, there is some evidence that the Labour Party has successful targeted groups of women voters. Less attention has been paid in the media to the targeting of men's votes but this research suggests that the Conservatives are more successful at recruiting the votes of younger men than younger women. Thus, political operatives should consider the full range of gender differences when identifying target groups.

Three questions about the relationship between gender and the vote in Britain were asked early on in this book. These were 1) Why gender dealignment in Britain?; 2) Is there evidence to support Norris's gender generation gap theory?;

and 3) If left-leaning political parties provide women-friendly platforms, is a modern gender gap likely to emerge in Britain to match the one currently evident in the United States? The conclusions presented so far help to provide some answers. Firstly gender dealignment in Britain appears to result from women's shift out of the home and into employment and higher education. Higher income mothers are now more likely to vote for the Labour party than older generations were and women's attitudes have shifted leftwards, with women prioritising spending on healthcare and education. There is evidence to support Norris's gender generation gap theory, particularly in political attitudes, but the gender generation gap varies according to electoral context. Thus we can draw some conclusions about question 3. The multiparty system in Britain and the recent attention paid by David Cameron's Conservatives to the representation of women and issues such as work life balance make it unlikely that a modern gender gap will emerge consistently election after election. What is more likely is that the parties will need to focus policies upon the issues that are prioritised by different groups of men and women in order to win their votes.

### THE STUDY OF WOMEN AND POLITICS

The research presented in this book contributes to the debate about the substantive and descriptive representation of women in politics. Differences were found in issue priority between men and women and differences in party identification and vote choice within sub-groups of men and women. Women in the surveys analysed were more likely to prioritise spending on health and education. Furthermore younger women were more likely to have feminist orientations than younger men. These finding complement an earlier elite level study of British politicians, where men and women politicians were found to have different attitudes towards women's issues, independent of party (Lovenduski and Norris 2004). As discussed in Chapters two and three, Anne Phillips argues that women may have interests that remain unarticulated in a male-dominated political system and that more women representatives are necessary if that interest is to be defined, voiced and acted upon. The research presented in this book, coupled with the elite-level study, provide some evidence of a nascent gendered political interest at the mass and elite levels, which may support one pillar of Anne Phillip's arguments for the equal representation of men and women,

### THE STUDY OF VOTING BEHAVIOUR

The early sections of this book highlighted the historic absence of systematic studies of gender and voting behaviour in Britain. The general approach has moved from a period when untested assumptions about sex differences were common, through a period when gender differences were ignored altogether, to the current time where sex is often included as a control variable but significant results are usually not discussed and are not explored further. The analysis presented here demonstrates that gender has a subtle and pervasive influence upon attitudes and behaviour that should be included in any comprehensive model of vote choice. The review of the United States gender gap literature highlighted the importance of utilising a concept of gender that includes subgroup analysis. Failing to consider differences between women and between men can undermine analysis by producing inflated predictions about potential differences between all men and all women, rather than the subtle interaction between sex and group membership that seems to provoke subgroup gender gaps. For example, in the United States, overall, women are more likely than men to support Democratic presidential candidates, but Southern religious women are more likely to be Republican identifiers than Southern religious men. Any attempt to model gender and vote that does not include subgroup analysis would fail to take account of these contradictory gender gaps. This book has demonstrated that there are significant differences between groups of men and women's political attitudes and behaviour; but these differences are complex and interact with other factors producing mixed results. It is crucial therefore that the sex/gender distinction is understood by researchers who include the sex variable in their analysis, and that theories of gender difference are incorporated into modelling processes, otherwise subtle and complex gender effects that influence behaviour and outcomes tend to be overlooked.

Recent debates about model heterogeneity may aid the inclusion of gender into the study of voting behaviour (Bartle 2005; Clarke *et al*. 2004). The one-size-fits-all approach does not allow for variation in the causal order and modelling variation in weight is complex and often unsatisfactory. John Bartle recommends the use of focus group research to 'provide valuable evidence about the language of politics at the mass level' (Bartle 2005: 671). He goes on to argue that 'such groups may suggest the "types" of voters that exist in the electorate' (*ibid*.). Bartle's recommendations are much in line with the approach of this book, which has used focus-group research and secondary data analysis to identify underlying gendered models of voting behaviour. It is hoped that the models of men and women's behaviour presented alongside each other in the preceding chapters illustrate that allowing for voter heterogeneity produces more insightful explanations than simply including background characteristics as control variables.

There have been major advances in the study of voting behaviour that allow us to consider the variety of motivators of vote choice, such as economic voting, issue salience, candidate evaluations and the effects of campaigning. What has been lacking is an account of what drives these variations. Developing models of voter heterogeneity that identify the differences in causal models across groups should help to address this shortfall. It is only when one appreciates the full complexity of the relationship between background characteristics, such as sex or gender, and vote that conclusions about their explanatory power can be made.

## NOTES

1   The study of gender, parenthood and vote has recently been furthered by pioneering research that has demonstrated that the sex of children influences the political attitude of parents. The parents of daughters were found to be more left-leaning than the parents of sons (Oswald and Powdthavee 2005). Thus, there is considerable scope for further analysis and it is important the widely accessible datasets include measures of parenthood.

2   In 2000, the average age of women in England and Wales at childbirth was 29.1 years (National Statistics: Social Trends 33).

# bibliography

Achen, C, 1992, 'Social psychology, demographic variables, and linear regression: breaking the iron triangle in voting research', *Political Behaviour* 14 (3): 195–211.

Almond, Gabriel, and Sidney Verba, 1963, *The Civic Culture: Political Attitudes and Democracy in Five Nations*, Princeton: Princeton University Press.

Almond, Gabriel, and Sidney Verba, 1980, *The Civic Culture Revisited*, London: Sage.

Andersen, Elizabeth, 2002, 'Should feminists reject rational choice theory?', in C. Witt (ed.) *A Mind of One's Own: Feminist Essays on Reason and Objectivity*, Boulder, Colorado: Westview Press.

Andersen, Kristi, 1999, 'The gender gap and experiences with the welfare state', *P.S.* 32 (1): 17–19.

Anzer, Christian, 2004, 'How rational is rational choice?', *European Political Science* 3 (2).

Bartle, John, 1998, 'Left-Right Position Matters, But Does Social Class? Causal Models of the 1992 British General Election', *British Journal of Political Science* 28: 501–529.

Bartle, John, 2005, 'Homogeneous models and heterogeneous voters', *Political Studies* 53 (4): 653–75.

Baxter, Sandra, and Marjorie Lansing, 1983, *Women and Politics: The Visible Majority*, Ann Arbor, Michigan: University of Michigan Press.

Bendyna, Mary, and Celinda Lake, 1994, 'Gender and voting in the '92 presidential elections', in A. Cook, S. Thomas and C. Wilcox, (eds.), *The Year of the Woman: Myths and Realities*, Boulder, San Francisco and Oxford: Westview Press.

Berelson, Bernard, Paul Lazarsfeld and William Mcphee, 1954, *Voting: A study of opinion formation in a presidential campaign*, Chicago: University of Chicago Press.

Berrington, Hugh, 2001, After the ball was over: the British general election of 2001, *European Politics* 24 (4): 206–215.

Bourque, Susan, and Jean Grossholtz, 1974, 'Politics an unnatural practice: political science looks at female participation', in Anne Phillips, (ed.), *Feminisim and Politics*, Oxford: Oxford University Press.

Box-Steffensmeir, Janet, Susan DeBoef, and Tse-Min Lin, 1997, 'Microideology, macropartisanship and the gender gap', paper read at American Political Science Association.

Bradshaw, Jonathan, Naomi Finch, Peter Kemp, Emese Mayhew and Julie Williams, 2003, Gender and poverty in Britain 'WPS', no. 6, London: Equal Opportunities Commission (EOC).

Butler, David and Donald Stokes, 1969, *Political Change in Britain*, 1st edition, London: Macmillan.

Butler, David, and Donald Stokes, 1974, *Political Change in Britain*, 2nd edition, London: Macmillan.

Campbell, Angus, Philip Converse, Warren Miller, and Donald Stokes, 1960, *The American Voter*, New York: John Wiley & Sons.

Campbell, Rosie, 2004, 'Gender, ideology and issue preference: is there such a thing as a political women's interest in Britain?', *British Journal of Politics and International Relations* 6: 20–46,

Campbell, Rosie, and Joni Lovenduski, 2005, 'Winning women's votes? The incremental track to equality', *Parliamentary Affairs* 58 (4).

Carroll, Susan, 1988, 'Women's autonomy and the gender gap: 1980 and 1982', in C. Mueller, (ed.), *The Politics of the Gender Gap*, Beverley Hills, California: Sage.

Carroll, Susan, 1999, 'The disempowerment of the gender gap: Soccer Moms and the 1996 elections', *P.S.* 32 (1):7–11.

Catt, Helena, 1996, 'Voting behaviour: a radical critique', in J. Townshend, (ed.), *Critical Political Studies*, London: Leicester University Press.

Chaney, Carole, Michael R. Alvarez and Jonathan Nagler, 1998, 'Explaining the gender gap in US presidential elections', *Political Research Quarterly* 51 (2).

Childs, Sarah, 2002, 'Hitting the target: are Labour women MPs "acting for" women?' *Parliamentary Affairs* 55 (1): 143–53.

Chodorow, Nancy, 1978, *The Reproduction of Mothering*, Berkeley, California: University of California Press.

Clark, Cal, and Janet Clark, 1986, 'Models of gender and political participation in the United States', *Women and Politics* 6: 5–25.

Clarke, Harold, Marianne Stewart, Mike Ault and Euel Elliott, 2004, 'Men, women and dynamics of presidential approval', *British Journal of Political Science* 35: 31–51.

Conover, Pamela, 1980, 'Comment: Rejoinder to Judd and Milburn', *American Sociological Review* 45 (4): 644–46.

Conover, Pamela, 1988, 'Feminists and the gender gap', *Journal of Politics* 50: 985–1010.

Converse, Phillip, 1964, 'The nature of belief systems in mass publics', in D. Apter, (ed.), *Ideology and Discontent*, New York: Free Press.

Crewe, Ivor, 1986, 'On the death and resurrection of class voting: some comments on how Britain votes', *Political Studies* XXXIV: 620.

Cudd, Ann, 2002, 'Rational choice theory and the lessons of feminism', in C. Witt, (ed.), *A Mind of One's Own: Feminist Essays on Reason and Objectivity*, Boulder, Colorado: Westview Press.

Dahlerup, Drude, 1988, 'From a small to a large minority: women in Scandinavian politics', *Scandinavian Political Studies* 11 (4).

Denver, David, and Gordon Hands, (eds.), 1992, *Issues and Controversies in British Electoral Behaviour*, London: Wheatsheaf.

Diamond, Irene, and Nancy Hartsock, 1981, 'Beyond interests in politics: A comment on Virginia Sapiro's "When are interests interesting? The problem of political representation of women"', *American Political Science Review* 75 (3): 717–21.

Dunleavy, Patrick, 1990, 'Mass political behaviour: is there more to learn?', *Political Studies* XXXVIII: 453–69.

Dunleavy, Patrick, and Christopher Husbands, 1985, *British Democracy at The Crossroads: Voting and Party Competition in the 1980s*, London: Allen and Unwin.

Duverger, Maurice, 1955, *The Political Role of Women*, Paris: UNESCO.

England, Paula, and Barbara Stanek Kilbourne, 1990a, 'Feminist critiques of the separative model of the self: implications for rational choice theory', *Rationality and Society* 2 (2):156–71.

England, Paula, and Barbara Stanek Kilbourne, 1990b, 'Does rational choice theory assume a separative self? Response to Friedman and Diem', *Rationality and Society* 2 (4): 522–5.

EOC, The, 2005, *Facts about Women and Men in Great Britain 2005*, The Equal Opportunities Commission.

Evans, Geoffrey, Anthony Heath, and Mansur Lalljee, 1996, 'Measuring left-right and libertarian-authoritarian values in the British electorate', *British Journal of Political Science* 47 (1): 94–112.

Feldman, Stanley, 1988, 'Structure and consistency in public opinion: the role of core beliefs and values', *American Journal of Political Science* 32 (2): 416–40.

Fenstermaker, Sarah, and Candice West, (eds.), 2002, *Doing Gender, Doing Difference: Inequality, Power, and Institutional Change*, New York: Routledge.

Fleishman, John, 1988, 'Attitude organisation in the general public: Evidence for a biodimensional structure', *Social Forces* 67 (1).

Franklin, Mark, 1985, *The Decline in Class Voting in Britain: Changes in the Base of Electoral Choice*, Oxford: Clarendon Press.

Frankovic, Kathleen, 1982, 'Sex and politics: new alignments, old issues', *P.S.* 15: 439–48.

Frazer, Elizabeth, and Ken Macdonald, 2003, 'Sex differences in political knowledge in Britain', *Political Studies* 51 (1): 67–83.

Gilligan, Carol, 1982, *In a Different Voice: Psychological Theory and Women's Development*, Cambridge, Massachusetts: Harvard University Press.

Goot, Murray, and Elizabeth Reid, 1975, *Women and Voting Studies: Mindless Matrons or Sexist Scientism?*, in R. Rose, (ed.) *Contemporary Political Sociology Series*, London: Sage.

Green, Donald, and Ian Shapiro, 1994, *Pathologies of Rational Choice Theory: A Critique of Applications in Political Science*, New Haven: Yale University Press.

Greenberg, Anna, 2001, 'Race, religiosity and the women's vote', *Women and*

*Politics* 22 (3).

Harding, Sandra, 1986, *The Science Question in Feminism*, Ithaca: Cornell University Press.

Harding, Sandra, 1991, *Whose Science? Whose Knowledge?*, Buckingham: Open University Press.

Harmen, Harriet, and Deborah Mattinson, 2000, *Winning for Women*, Fabian Society.

Harrop, Martin, 2001, An apathetic landslide: the British election of 2001, *Government and Opposition* (3): 295–313.

Hartmann, Heidi, 1981, 'The family as the locus of gender, class and political struggle', *Signs* 6: 366–94.

Hayes, Bernadette, 1997, 'Gender, feminism and electoral behaviour in Britain', *Electoral Studies* 16 (2): 203–16.

Hayes, Bernadette, and Clive Bean, 1993, 'Gender and local political interest', *Political Studies* 41 (4): 672–82.

Heath, Anthony, John Curtice, Roger Jowell, Geoffrey Evans, Julia Field and Sharon Witherspoon, 1991, *Understanding political change: The British Voter: 1964–1987*, Oxford: Pergamon.

Heath, Anthony, Geoffrey Evans and Jean Martin, 1993, 'The measurement of core beliefs and values: the development of balanced socialist/laissez faire and libertarian/authoritarian scales', *British Journal of Political Science* 24: 115–58.

Heath, Anthony, Roger Jowell and John Curtice, 1985, *How Britain Votes*, Oxford: Oxford University Press.

Heath, Anthony, Roger Jowell and John Curtice, 1987, 'Trendless fluctuation: a reply to Crewe', *Political Studies* XXXV: 256–77.

Hooks, Bell, 1982, *Ain't I a Woman? Black Women and Feminism*, London: Pluto Press.

Hooks, Bell, 1989, *Talking Back: Thinking Feminist Thinking Black*, Toronto: Between the Lines.

Inglehart, Ronald, and Pippa Norris, 1999, 'The developmental theory of the gender gap: women and men's voting behaviour in global perspective', *International Political Science Review* 21 (4): 441–462.

Inglehart, Ronald, 1977, *The Silent Revolution: Changing Values and Political Styles among Western Publics*, Princeton, New Jersey: Princeton University Press.

Inglehart, Ronald, and Pippa Norris, 2000, 'The developmental theory of the gender gap: women and men's voting behaviour in global perspective', *International Political Science Review*, 21 (4): 441–63.

Jaccard, James, Robert Turrisi and Choi Kwan, 1996, *Interaction Effects in Multiple Regression*, London: Sage.

Jelen, Ted, Sue Thomas and Clyde Wilcox, 1994, 'The gender gap in comparative perspective: gender differences in abstract ideology and concrete issues in Western Europe', *European Journal of Political Research* 25: 171–86.

Jennings, M. Kent, and Barbara Farah, 1980, 'Ideology, gender and political action: a cross-national survey', *British Journal of Political Science* 10 (2): 219–40.

Judd, C., J. Krosnick and M. Milburn, 1981, 'Political involvement and attitude structure in the general public', *American Sociological Review* 46 (5): 660–9.

Judd, C., and M. Milburn, 1980, 'The structure of attitude systems in the general public: Comparisons of a structural equation model', *American Sociological Review* 45 (4): 627–43.

Karvonen, Laura, and Per Selle, (eds.), 1995, *Women in Nordic Politics: Closing the Gap*, Brookfield: Dartmouth.

Kaufmann, Karen, and John Petrocik, 1999, 'The changing politics of American men: Understanding the sources of the gender gap', *American Journal of Political Science* 43 (3): 864–997.

Kenski, Kate, and Kathleen Hall Jamieson, 2000, 'The gender gap in political knowledge', in K. Hall, (ed.), *Everything You Need Know About Politics... And Why You Are Wrong*, Jamieson, New York: Basic Books.

Kornhauser, Marjorie, 1987, 'The rhetoric of the anti-progressive income tax movement: a typical male reaction', *Michigan Law Review* 86: 465–523.

Kornhauser, Marjorie, 1997, 'What do women want? Feminism and the progressive income tax', *American University Law Review* 47 (1): 151–63.

Lijphart, Arend, 1980, 'The structure of inference', in G. Almond and S. Verba, (eds.), *The Civic Culture Revisited*, London: Sage.

Lipset, Seymour Martin, 1960, *Political Man*, Baltimore: Johns Hopkins University Press.

Lovenduski, Joni, 1998, 'Gendering research in political science', *Annual Review of Political Science* 1: 333–56.

Lovenduski, Joni, 2001, 'Gender and politics: critical mass or minority representation', in Pippa Norris, (ed.), *Britain Votes 2001*, Oxford: Oxford University Press.

Lovenduski, Joni, and Pippa Norris, 2004, 'Westminster women: the politics of presence', *Political Studies* 51 (1): 84–102.

Manza, Jeff, and Clem Brooks, 1998, 'The gender gap in US presidential elections: When? why? implications?' *American Journal of Sociology* 103 (5).

Mattei, Laura, and Franco Mattei, 1998, 'If men stayed at home: The gender gap and recent congressional elections', *Political Research Quarterly* 5 (2).

Miller, Arthur, Martin Wattenberg and Okasana Malanchuk, 1996, 'Schematic assessments of presidential candidates', *American Political Science Review* 80 (2): 521–540.

Miller, Warren E., and Levitan, Teresa E., 1976, *The New Politics and the American Electorate*, Cambridge, MA: Winthrop Publishers.

Miller, Warren, and Merrill J. Shanks, 1996, *The New American Voter*, Cambridge: Harvard University Press.

Mondak, Jeffery, and Mary Anderson, 2004, 'The knowledge gap: a reexamination of gender-based differences in political knowledge', *Journal of Politics* 66 (2): 492–512.

Mueller, Carol (ed.), 1988, *The Politics of the Gender Gap*, Vol. 12, Sage Yearbooks in Women's Policy Studies, Beverly Hills: Sage.

Nie, Norman, Sidney Verba and John Petrocik, 1979, *The Changing American Voter*, Cambridge, Massachusetts: Harvard University Press.

Norris, Pippa, 1997, *Electoral Change Since 1945*, Oxford: Blackwell.

Norris, Pippa, 1999, 'Gender: a gender-generation gap?', in G. Evans and Pippa Norris (eds.), *Critical Elections: British Parties and Voters in Long-Term Perspective*, London: Sage.

Norris, Pippa, 2001, 'The gender gap: old challenges, new approaches', in S. Carroll, (ed.), *Women and American Politics: Agenda Setting for the 21st Century*, Oxford: Oxford University Press.

Norris, Pippa, Joni Lovenduski, and Rosie Campbell, 2004, *Gender and Political Participation*, London: The Electoral Commission.

Oakely, Ann, 1972, *Sex, Gender and Society*, London: Temple Smith.

O'Brien, Margaret, and Ian Shemilt, 2003, *Working Fathers*, University of East Anglia: EOC.

Oswald, Andrew, and Nattavudh Powdthavee, 2005, *Daughters and Left-Wing Voting*, Working Paper, www.oswald.co.uk.

Pateman, Carole, 1980, 'The civic culture: a philosophical critique', in G. Almond and S. Verba, (eds.), *The Civic Culture Revisited*, London: Sage.

Phillips, Anne, 1994, 'The case for gender parity, or why should it matter who our representatives are?', *Swiss Yearbook of Political Science*.

Phillips, Anne, 1995, *The Politics of Presence*, Oxford: Oxford University Press.

Pitkin, Hannah, 1967, *The Concept of Representation*, Berkeley: University of California Press.

Randall, Vicky, 1991, *Feminism and Political Analysis*, Political Studies 39.

Rose, Richard, and Ian McAllister, 1986, *Voters Begin to Choose*, London: Sage.

Ruddick, Sara, 1989, *Maternal Thinking*, Boston: Beacon Press.

Sanders, David, 1991, 'Government and popularity and the next general election', *Political Quarterly* 62: 235–61.

Sanders, David, 1996, 'Economic performance, management competence and the outcome of the next general election', *Political Studies* 44: 203–31.

Sanders, David, Harold Clarke, Marriane Stewart and Paul Whiteley, 2001, 'The Economy and Voting', in P. Norris (ed.) *Britain Votes 2001*, Oxford: Oxford University Press.

Sanders, David, 1999, 'The impact of left-right ideology', in G. Evans and Pippa Norris (eds.), *Critical Elections: British Voters and Parties in Long-Term Perspective*, London: Sage.

Sanders, David, Hugh Ward and David Marsh, 1991, 'Macroeconomics, the Falklands War and the popularity of the Thatcher government: a contrary view', in H. Norpoth, M. Lewis-Beck and J. D. Lafay, *Economics and Politics*, Ann Arbor, MI: University of Michigan Press.

Sapiro, Virginia, 1983, *The Political Integration of Women*, Urbana: University of Illinois Press.

Sapiro, Virginia, and Pamela Conover, 1997, 'The variable gender basis of electoral politics: gender and context in the 1992 US Election', *British Journal of Political Science* 27 (4): 497–523.

Särlvik, Bo, and Ivor Crewe, 1983, *Decade of Dealignment: The Conservative Victory of 1979 and Electoral Trends in the 1970s*, Cambridge: Cambridge University Press.

Scarbrough, Elinor, 2000, 'The British Election Study', *Political Studies* 48: 391–414.

Scott, John, Richard Matland, Phillip Michelbach, and Brian Bornstein, 2001, 'Just deserts: An experimental study of distributive justice norms', *American Journal of Political Science* 45 (4): 749–67.

Seltzer, Richard, Jody Newman and Melissa Leighton, 1997, *Sex as a Political Variable: Women as Candidates and Voters in U.S. Elections*, Boulder, Colorado: Lynne Rienner Publishers, Inc.

Shapiro, Robert, and Harpreet Mahajan, 1986, 'Gender differences in policy preferences: a summary of trends from the 1960s to the 1980s', *Public Opinion Quarterly* 50 (1): 42–61.

Squires, Judith and Mark Wickham-Jones, 2001, 'Women in Parliament: A Comparative Analysis', Equal Opportunities Commission (EOC).

Steel, Gill, 2003, 'Class and gender in British general elections', Paper prepared for the presentation at the Midwest Political Science Association Annual Meeting, Chicago.

Stephenson, Mary-Ann, 1998, *The Glass Trapdoor: Women, Politics and the Media During the 1997 General Election*, London: Fawcett.

Stokes, Donald, 1996, 'Some dynamic elements of contests for the presidency', *American Political Science Review* 60 (1): 19–28.

Tingsten, H, 1937, *Political Behaviour: Studies in Election Statistics*, London: P.S. King.

Wängnerud, Lena, 2000, 'Testing the politics of presence: women's representation in the Swedish Riksdag', *Scandinavian Political Studies* 23 (1): 67–91.

Ware, Alan, 1990, 'Meeting needs through voluntary action: does market society corrode altruism?', in Alan Ware and Robert Goodin, (eds.), *Needs and Welfare*, London: Sage.

Welch, Susan, 1977, 'Women as political animals? A test of some explanations of male-female political participation differences', *American Journal of Political Science* 21: 711–30.

Welch, Susan, and John Hibbing, 1992, 'Financial conditions, gender and voting in American national elections', *American Politics Quarterly* 21: 343–59.

Whiteley, Paul, Harold Clarke, David Sanders and Marriane Stewart, 2001, 'Turnout' in P. Norris (ed.), *Britain Votes 2001*, Oxford: Oxford University Press

Wirls, Daniel, 1986, 'Reinterpreting the gender gap', *Public Opinion Quarterly* 50

(3): 316–330.

Withey, Julie, 2003, *Redefining Gender Gaps: Political Behaviour through the Changing Lens of Gender*, London: Guildhall University.

# index

# Also available from the ECPR Press

Representing Women?
Female legislators in West
European Parliaments

Mercedes Mateo Diaz

April 2005
234mmx156mm / 276pp
Pb: 978-0-9547966-4-8
£22.00

This book examines political participation, representation and legitimacy in the national parliaments of European Union countries. Organised around three major questions: what affects women's presence in parliaments?, does the number of women in a parliament have an effect?, and do women in parliaments represent women?, the author argues that, to be effective, institutional reforms need a 'minimal environment' with respect to socio-economic factors. Contrary to critical mass theory, which claims that a small number of representatives cannot have much impact on political outcomes, it seems that smaller groups of women can influence various aspects of the legislative process. The author argues that an electoral system's level of proportionality influences the extent to which parliaments and assemblies mirror their populations both socially and ideologically.

**Place an order at www.ecprnet.org**